Southwest
INDIAN COUNTRY

ARIZONA, NEW MEXICO, SOUTHERN UTAH AND COLORADO

By the Editors of Sunset Books and Sunset Magazine

D1275345

Lane Books · Menlo Park, California

FOREWORD

Southwest Indian Country is a region of lonely mesas, barren deserts, and weirdly eroded pinnacles, craters, and natural arches. Stark volcanic cones tower above pastel sands. Rivers rage deep in canyons whose vertical walls reveal layered chapters of geologic history harkening back to the very beginnings of life on this planet.

This is a primitive land of burning sun and turquoise-blue sky. Piles of billowing white clouds tower above forested mountain peaks. Black thunderheads sweep across the plain on a summer afternoon, wind whips the sands into spiraling dust devils, and flash floods drench the dry earth. Then a vivid rainbow signals the end of the passing storm. The lengthening shadows of monumentlike buttes and spires move silently across the storm-washed sand, ushering in a fiery sunset and chilled evening.

The overpowering character of the land is reflected in the life and art of its people. Meeting the challenge of their harsh environment shaped the social order and mythology of each Southwest Indian group. Ceremonial art and ritual represent means of dealing with the powerful forces of nature that surround them.

Only a strong and adaptive people could survive the challenge of this environment for so many thousands of years. They continue to survive by adapting to the new challenges that crowd in upon their lives. These people and the dramatic character of their land make this one of the most fascinating regions of the West.

Photographers

WILLIAM APLIN: pages 54, 56, 61 (left), 67 (right); GLENN CHRISTIANSEN: pages 9 (left), 15, 16, 22-23, 30, 32, 58, 60, 61 (right), 68, 71. RICHARD DAWSON: pages 8 (right), 10, 31 (left), 36, 42, 48 (right), 49 (left), 67 (left); PHYLLIS ELVING: pages 7, 28 (top right), 43, 48 (left), 49 (right), 50, 75; JICARILLA APACHE TRIBE: page 65; OLIVER JOHNSON: page 31 (right); WILL KIRKMAN: page 21; MARTIN LITTON: pages 77, 78; NATIONAL PARK SERVICE: page 74; NEW MEXICO STATE TOURIST BUREAU: pages 8 (left), 47; RALPH POOLE: page 72; HAL ROTH: page 53; LARRY SMITH: page 27 (left); DARROW WATT: page 45; R. WENKAM: pages 9 (right), 12, 19, 24, 25, 28 (top left, bottom); MERRILL WINDSOR: pages 22-23, 27 (right); JOHN V. YOUNG: page 63.

FRONT COVER: Navajo family drives flock of sheep across dunes of Monument Valley on the Navajo Indian Reservation. In the background are some of the sandstone formations that give the area its name. Photograph by Josef Muench.

BACK COVER: Masked crown dancers escort buckskin-clad Apache maidens in annual All-Indian Pow Wow parade in Flagstaff, Arizona. Photograph by Robert Wenkam.

ILLUSTRATIONS by Dinah James.
MAPS by Susan Lampton.

CONTENTS

Special Features

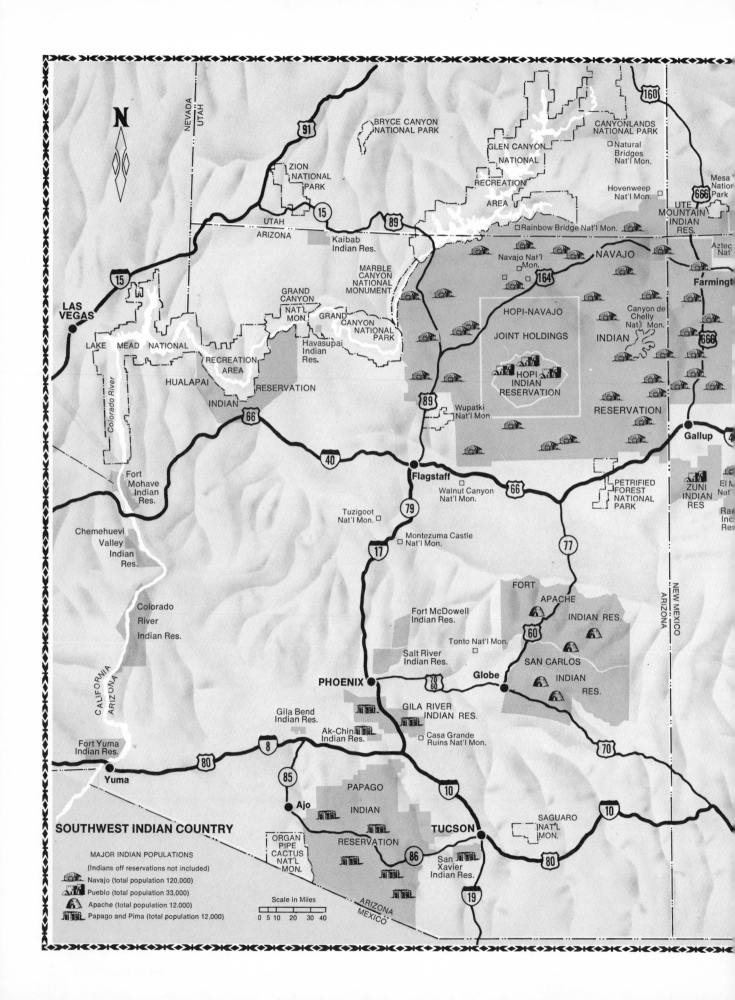

N

NEVADA / UTAH

⑨①

BRYCE CANYON
NATIONAL PARK

CANYONLANDS
NATIONAL PARK

GLEN CANYON

NATIONAL

RECREATION

AREA

☐ Natural
Bridges
Nat'l Mon.

☐ Hovenweep
Nat'l Mon.

⑯⓿

Mesa
Natior
Park

ZION
NATIONAL
PARK

⑮

⑧⑨

☐ Rainbow Bridge Nat'l Mon.

UTE
MOUNTAIN
INDIAN
RES.

UTAH

ARIZONA

Kaibab
Indian Res.

Navajo Nat'l
☐ Mon.

NAVAJO

Aztec
Nat'

⑮

MARBLE
CANYON
NATIONAL
MONUMENT

⑯④

Farmingt

LAS
VEGAS

GRAND
CANYON
NAT'L
MON.

GRAND
CANYON
NATIONAL
PARK

HOPI-NAVAJO

JOINT HOLDINGS

INDIAN

Canyon de
Chelly
Nat'l Mon.

⑥⑥⑥

LAKE   MEAD   NATIONAL

Havasupai
Indian
Res.

HOPI
INDIAN
RESERVATION

RESERVATION

Colorado River

RECREATION
AREA

HUALAPAI

INDIAN

RESERVATION

Wupatki
Nat'l Mon.

⑧⑨

⑥⑥

Gallup

④

Fort
Mohave
Indian
Res.

⑥⑥

④⓿

Flagstaff

Walnut Canyon
Nat'l Mon.

⑥⑥

PETRIFIED
FOREST
NATIONAL
PARK

ZUNI
INDIAN
RES

El M
Nat'

Chemehuevi
Valley
Indian
Res.

⑦⑨

Tuzigoot
Nat'l Mon. ☐

Montezuma Castle
☐ Nat'l Mon.

⑰

⑦⑦

Ra
Inc
Res

Colorado
River
Indian Res.

FORT

APACHE

INDIAN RES.

NEW MEXICO

ARIZONA

Fort McDowell
Indian Res.

Tonto Nat'l Mon.
☐

⑥⓿

CALIFORNIA

ARIZONA

Salt River
Indian Res.

SAN CARLOS

Fort Yuma
Indian Res.

PHOENIX

⑦⓿
⑥⓿

Globe

INDIAN

RES.

⑧⓿

⑧

⑧⓿

Yuma

⑧⑤

GILA RIVER
INDIAN RES.

☐ Casa Grande
Ruins Nat'l Mon.

⑦⓿

Gila Bend
Indian Res.

Ak-Chin
Indian Res.

Ajo

PAPAGO

INDIAN

⑩

SAGUARO
NAT'L
MON.

⑩

SOUTHWEST INDIAN COUNTRY

ORGAN
PIPE
CACTUS
NAT'L
MON.

RESERVATION

TUCSON

⑧⓿

⑧⑥

San
Xavier
Indian Res.

Scale in Miles

0 5 10   20   30   40

ARIZONA
MEXICO

⑲

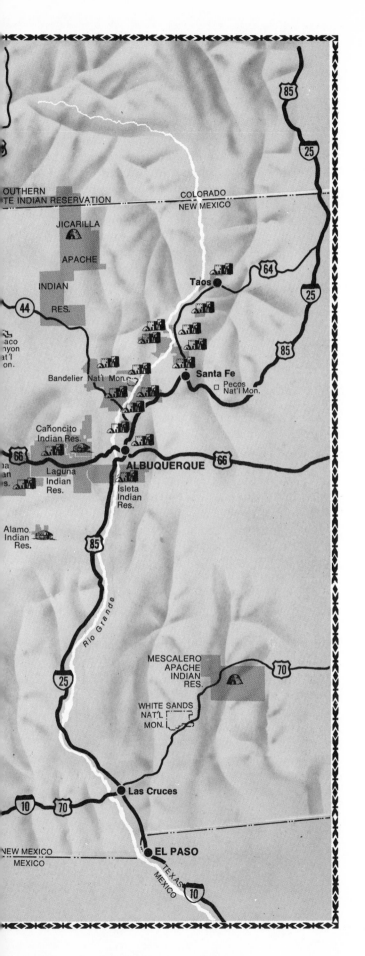

DISCOVERING INDIAN COUNTRY

Only a few miles from the activity of a modern Southwest city, you can find yourself encompassed by a vast, still landscape. The land stretches out for miles around you, blanketed in colors sometimes vivid, sometimes muted, and empty of any visible human habitation. Yet in this country are the largest centers of Indian population in the United States.

Traveling through this dramatic section of the Southwest—much of Arizona and New Mexico and the southern part of Colorado and Utah—is a fascinating way to learn about Indian cultures that have retained distinctive tribal characteristics long after most other North American tribes have been absorbed by modern society.

This is an area rich in archeological relics, too, providing insight into the way surprisingly advanced civilizations lived here a thousand years ago. Seeing the land, harsh and unyielding for all its beauty, makes you aware of how amazing their achievements were. You have the feeling man could walk across this country without leaving any footprints at all, yet those left by the prehistoric Indians are remarkably readable today.

The scenery itself is what keeps drawing many travelers back to Indian country. Towering buttes, cliffs, and chimney rocks form impressive skylines in the canyon-plateau country that makes up a large part of the area, while saguaros stand sentry nearer the Mexican border. Color is a memorable part of your impressions of this land. Oftentimes it is subdued—the greens grayed, the mountains a blue haze in the distance. Almost everywhere there is a red cast to the earth —from a slight pink to a deep rust.

In this setting live 170,000 Indians, the majority on reservations. The Navajos are the most populous tribe in the United States and have the largest reservation, some 16,000,000 acres in northeast Arizona, northwest New Mexico, and southeast Utah. Nineteen separate Pueblo groups are located in New Mexico; the Hopis are a pueblo-dwelling "island" surrounded by Navajo lands in Arizona. Apaches live on reservations in both New Mexico and Arizona. Other Arizona Indians include the Papago, Pima, Paiute, Chemehuevi, Cocopah, Mohave, Havasupai, Hualapai, Yavapai, Maricopa, and Yuma tribes. Ute Indians live in southern Colorado and northern New Mexico.

THE EARLY CULTURES

The Navajos and the Apaches are relative newcomers to the Southwest. They are descendents of Athabaskan bands who came from the North sometime between the years 1000 and 1500. The Spaniards, who arrived in 1539, used *Apache* as a general term which included both the Navajos and the Apaches, distinguishing individual bands as *Apache de Navajo, Apache de Jicarilla,* and so on. Eventually the word *Navajo* was used alone as the name of a group separate from the Apaches.

Traditionally hunters and gatherers, the Navajos learned weaving and farming from Pueblo Indian neighbors and became semi-nomadic herdsmen when the Spaniards brought horses, sheep, and goats to the Southwest. Horses also increased the scope of Navajo and Apache raids on Indian and Spanish settlements. The Apaches, more influenced by Plains Indians than were their Navajo cousins, maintained a nomadic life of hunting and raiding.

Long before the Athabaskans arrived, pueblo-dwelling Indians had established their culture in the Southwest. In fact, the name given these ancestors of today's Pueblo Indians is the Navajo word *Anasazi*—"the ancient ones." They built the great prehistoric cities of the Southwest, then mysteriously abandoned most of them by the end of the thirteenth century. Tales of these multi-storied "apartment-house" dwellings led the Spaniards to believe they held fabulous wealth and prompted Coronado's 1540 expedition in search of the legendary Seven Cities of Cibola. The Spaniards found no storehouses of gold or jewels, only agricultural communities which

they called *pueblos,* Spanish for "villages"— hence the name Pueblo Indians. Actually the Pueblos, while they share a common cultural heritage, are not tribally related. Each pueblo was established as an independent entity, and even language differs from one to another.

The Papago and Pima Indians of southern Arizona are believed by many archeologists to be descendants of a culture that reached its peak even earlier than that of the pueblo-building Anasazi. Called *Hohokam* from a Pima word for "those who have vanished," their achievements included the construction of an extensive system of irrigation canals thought to have been well developed by 700 A.D. Today the Papagos live primarily on a large reservation west of Tucson; the Pimas live near Phoenix.

The ancestors of the American Indian tribes did not originate on this continent. The most commonly accepted theory of how they got here is that they came from Asia by way of the Bering Strait in a series of many migrations thousands of years ago. A more fascinating explanation is the Indian legend that the people emerged from underground into the Southwest.

TRADITION AND MODERN SOCIETY

Indian life today is a study in contrasts. Some of them are easily visible—pueblo dwellings with glass windows and television sets; lonely adobe hogans a few miles from industrial centers; women in traditional tribal dress walking down modern city streets. Old and new ways jostle up against one another. Traditionalists cling to old customs; younger leaders urge acceptance of progressive ways as they try both to preserve their Indian heritage and benefit from modern society.

Non-Indian dress, food, architecture, and language have been adopted to such an extent in some Indian communities that little remains to distinguish them from any other Southwest towns. In other places Indian life has remained relatively unchanged over the years.

Some outsiders dismiss any change in old patterns as not being truly "Indian." Yet from the earliest times Indians have adapted elements of the different cultures with which they came in contact. Indians are famous for silverwork, but they did not learn that craft until midway through the nineteenth century. The Navajo woman's "traditional" dress style dates from the post-Civil War period when such clothing was

NEW-STYLE *Navajo hogan has windows, sloping wood roof. Old-style hogans are flat-roofed and windowless.*

issued during a long captivity at Fort Sumner, New Mexico. Even beadwork, which many people think of as the most authentically Indian craft of all, was unknown to the Indians before the coming of the Spaniards.

The tribal governments

The Indian has three political identities. In addition to being a United States citizen and a state resident, he is a member of a tribe. (He also may be a member of still another group, a clan.) Tribal governments have gradually taken over many functions formerly administered by the Bureau of Indian Affairs, whose agencies are responsible for providing some of the same services that non-Indians receive from federal, state, and local governments.

The tribe's governing body usually is a tribal council. The largest of these is the democratically elected 74-member Navajo council, which meets at Window Rock, Arizona. This lively legislature has initiated such programs as building housing projects and community centers, running motels, operating a sawmill, and establishing a tribal park system. Similar enterprises have been undertaken by other tribes, notably the White Mountain Apaches.

Progress has been made in meeting such problems as disease and illiteracy, but they continue to plague the Indian. The tuberculosis rate among Indians is much higher than among non-Indians, and the average life expectancy is shorter. The U.S. Public Health Service operates hospitals and clinics on the reservations, and a number of church groups have established hospitals for the Indians.

Indian children attend public, government, and church schools. Often they must leave home and attend boarding schools; today tribal governments and the Bureau of Indian Affairs are trying to establish schools closer to home. The rate of attendance is increasing, though there is still a high dropout rate. Tribal governments recognize the importance of education, and several tribes have set up funds for college and vocational school scholarships. The Navaho Community College, which opened in 1969 at Many Farms, Arizona, is the first college to be located on an Indian reservation and run by Indians.

SHOPPING FOR INDIAN CRAFTWORK

Since the time of the first Spanish conquistadors, travelers to the Southwest have been fascinated by the skill of Indian craftsmen. Work of fine quality still is produced, and it is one excellent reason for visiting this land and its people.

The importance of nature in the Indian's culture probably helped develop his ability to use natural materials, colors, and forms. From early times he displayed a sophisticated sense of design. New materials, techniques, and design influences have been absorbed from each new culture the Indians have contacted over the centuries. The work of each tribe or group has developed certain characteristics, though there is never one "authentic" tribal style. Sometimes a single artist's work becomes so well known that it is thought of as the "typical" style of his group.

Rugs, baskets, pottery, jewelry

The beautiful handwoven rugs made by the Navajos are among the most famous of Indian-made articles. Though the Navajos learned weaving from Pueblo Indians, little weaving is done by Pueblos today; Hopi Indians do weave sashes and other ceremonial apparel. The related art of basket-weaving is concentrated primarily among the Papagos and the Hopis. Pima and Apache tribes once made fine baskets but today produce only small quantities.

Pottery, produced in the coil method rather than with a potter's wheel, is made by the Hopis and by many Pueblo groups. Pottery-making was highly developed more than a thousand years ago, and each region and period of time was characterized by a particular style. Pottery fragments therefore have helped archeologists put together the story of the prehistoric Indians. The introduction of metal pots by the Spaniards almost destroyed the practice of pottery-making in Pueblo villages. Anthropologists were instrumental in reviving the art.

The silver and turquoise jewelry of the Zunis, Navajos, and Hopis is well known. Turquoise has been used for centuries, but silver work did not begin until the nineteenth century. Silver is the dominant element in Navajo jewelry, while Zuni work emphasizes the stones and often includes shell, jet, and coral in a mosaic of various colors. Recently the Hopis have developed their own distinctive styles utilizing traditional Hopi pottery designs.

NAVAJO WEAVER doesn't draw pattern for rug but works from mental conception of finished design.

PUEBLO POTTER from village of San Ildefonso skillfully works clay to prepare pot for firing.

Judging quality work

High quality in Indian craftwork is encouraged by such institutions as museums and tribal arts and crafts organizations. Of course, there are plenty of "Indian curios" of inferior quality—including many made commercially and imported to the Southwest. You will soon learn to distinguish the shops specializing in these from places that emphasize genuine Indian products. Compare machine-made imitations with Indian handmade articles. Dealers in reputable Indian art shops and museum stores are willing to guarantee the authenticity of their wares.

Excellent displays of both ancient and modern Indian products at museums throughout the Southwest can be of great help in developing your eye for Indian art. The more you learn about Indian crafts, the more wisely you will be able to shop and the more completely you will enjoy your purchases. Knowing that a Hopi woman may spend a whole day weaving just one and a half coils of a basket increases your appreciation of the beautifully woven plaque you take home.

A few simple checks for quality can tell you a great deal. Rub your finger across the design on a piece of pottery; the paint shouldn't rub off.

When you shop for a handwoven rug, put it on the floor to check that corners do not curl, that there are no wrinkles, and that edges are straight. Pry apart the fibers to check the warp—it should be wool, not cotton.

Prices vary according to the quality of the article and the reputation of the artist. Art dealers and collectors from all over the world tour this country regularly, and Indian craftsmen are now well aware of the value of their work. Trying to bargain over price isn't likely to be effective.

Shops along the main thoroughfares and temporary booths at fairs and festivals make crafts easily accessible, but be cautious when you shop. Some places thrive on a careless tourist market.

Other places where you will find crafts include trading posts, homes or shops of craftsmen, special crafts shows at museums, and tribally sponsored stores. A number of tribes have cooperative associations through which crafts are sold. These often offer an excellent variety of top-quality work, and you can be assured of the authenticity of the articles they sell; do not expect prices to be lower, however. Some craftsmen who sell through cooperatives also have their own direct sales outlets, but there are others whose work can be purchased only through the cooperatives.

HOPI woman weaves yucca strips around grass filler for coiled basket. Papagos also make baskets.

KACHINA DOLLS made by Hopis are carved from roots of cottonwood trees, then brightly painted.

DANCERS pantomime movements of deer during feast day celebration at Nambe pueblo. Most Indian dances are religious rituals.

VISITING THE RESERVATIONS

When you travel on Indian lands, be sure to observe rules of courtesy and comply with reservation regulations. In many places there are rules regarding photography, and it is *very* important that you follow them. Cameras are forbidden on the Hopi mesas. New Mexico's Pueblo villages have individual regulations; put away your camera before you enter a village, and find out what the regulations are before you take any pictures or do any sketching or painting. Some of the more conservative villages prohibit all photography, while most issue a special photographer's permit for a small fee (frequently higher on feast days and other special occasions). On Navajo, Papago, and Apache reservations no photo permit is required. However, here and in the pueblos, common courtesy demands that you request permission before taking anybody's photograph, and a small payment usually is expected.

When you enter a Pueblo village, the first thing you should do is to call on its governor or his representative. He will explain any tourist fees, outline photography restrictions, point out the homes and shops of craftsmen, and tell you the dates and hours of festivals.

On other reservations, tribal offices are good sources of information. The federal government's Indian Agency offices also can provide answers to your questions.

Ceremonials and special events

Colorful Indian ceremonials, festivals, and dances take place throughout the year. Visitors are extended the privilege of attending many of them, as long as they abide by the established ground rules. Never take photographs or even make notes without asking permission. Be as unobtrusive as possible and in no way interfere with any ceremonial procedures. Most Indian dances are religious observances, and you must show proper respect for them.

While some major ceremonials are scheduled well ahead of time, there are many that are planned only a short time in advance. Your chances of seeing some sort of ceremony are especially good during the summer months; check with tribal offices or chambers of commerce when you are in an area to find out what events may be taking place while you are there.

A complete listing of major events that are scheduled ahead is given in the American Indian Calendar prepared by the Bureau of Indian Affairs. To obtain a copy, send 30 cents to the Superintendent of Documents, U.S. Government Printing Office, Washington, D.C. 20402.

GUIDES FOR THE TRAVELER

When you travel in the Southwest, you have your choice of desert or mountain climate. You can speed over freeways or explore dirt roads, and you can stay in a modern resort or make camp in a primitive wilderness area.

Climate in the Southwest

The dry climate of the Southwest has enabled archeologists to learn a great deal about its early inhabitants. Because decay is arrested if conditions are arid enough, much material from prehistoric days has remained intact over the centuries, including house timbers which archeologists have been able to date by the tree-ring method.

Actually there is quite a wide variation in climate, since Indian country encompasses both low elevations and high plateaus and mountains. In the southern desert area, summer temperatures climb into the 100's, and winters are warm and sunny. In high elevations warm summer days turn crisp at night, and winters may be severe. Travel conditions in the northern regions are best from late April through October; in the southern desert, winter months are most pleasant. Showers are most frequent in July and August throughout the Southwest, but winter storms are not uncommon. There may be winter snow in some areas.

Driving conditions

Paved highways span much of the Indian country. Interstate 40 is the main east-west through route, connecting Flagstaff, Gallup, and Albuquerque as it crosses Arizona and New Mexico; for much of the way it follows old U.S. Highway 66. Interstate 8 and 10 provide a southern route.

Interstate 25 is a north-south route through New Mexico and Colorado. Other good highways join once-remote areas.

Traveling through the back country can be the most fun. Principal gravel and dirt roads usually are well maintained. Others have little traffic and should not be traveled by anyone not equipped for emergencies. Some are impassable in wet weather. Inquire locally about road conditions.

Much reservation land is open range for cattle and sheep; watch out for livestock on the road. In some places water fills dips in the road after rainstorms—there may or may not be signs warning you of flash flood areas.

Accommodations

As overnight accommodations on the Indian reservations are limited, it is wise to make reservations ahead or plan to stay in nearby communities. New motels, restaurants, and resorts are being planned on a number of reservations as tribes undertake increased tourism development.

Some resort areas in the Southwest operate on a seasonal basis and are closed during the off season—winter in the northern regions, summer in the south.

Camping on reservation land

The Indian reservations provide excellent camping opportunities, from well developed campgrounds to unimproved backcountry sites. In many places a tribal camping permit is required. See the section on camping in each chapter for specific information about fees, regulations, and campgrounds.

Hunting and fishing

Most reservations allow hunting and fishing by non-Indians, but you must have a tribal permit in addition to a state license. See the section on a specific reservation for further information.

Deer are found in most forested regions. Other game animals are elk, antelope, black bears, javelinas (wild pigs), bighorn sheep, wild turkeys, wildcats, coyotes, and mountain lions. There is waterfowl, quail, and dove hunting in some areas.

Hundreds of miles of trout streams cross reservation lands. You also can fish for black bass, channel catfish, and crappie.

NAVAJO TERRITORY

Also the Hopis...Hualapais...Havasupais

The Navajos' name for themselves is simply *Dineh*—the People. They number 120,000 (compared to 16,000 a century ago) and their reservation stretches over 16½ million acres of deep canyons, strange rock formations, vast open spaces, forested mountains, and dry mesas. A journey to their land offers glimpses of more ancient cultures as well; surrounded by the Navajo reservation are the pueblos of the Hopi Indians, and across the whole region are relics left by the pueblo dwellers who lived here 1,000 years ago.

While the Navajo tribe has been progressive in accepting modern methods of improving the standard of living on their reservation, many of the traditional patterns of life still are followed. More than ninety per cent speak the native Navajo language fluently—many of them speak only this language. The long skirts and richly colored velveteen blouses adopted by Navajo women a hundred years ago are still much in evidence. And many of the Navajos continue to live in isolated hogans made of mud and logs with earthen floors, or new-style with windows and slanted wooden roofs. Navajos have never settled in communities, and it is unusual to find more than two or three hogans together. Recently, as industry has begun to develop on the reservation, a few communities have been established around centers

of employment. But most of the names on a map of the Navajo reservation still are simply trading posts, sometimes with a school nearby.

Tribal development

Little is known of early Navajo history. At some point between 1000 and 1500 A.D. the Athabascan ancestors of today's Navajos migrated to the Southwest in small bands from farther north. Some historians feel they had only recently arrived when the Spaniards came in the mid-1500's, while others feel they may have been here several centuries earlier. The presence of such groups of hunters and raiders might help explain why the Pueblo people abandoned their great cities in the Four Corners area by the beginning of the fourteenth century.

After the Spaniards came, the Navajos acquired horses and sheep—and a pattern of life that many still follow. During Spanish and Mexican rule the Navajos never were conquered, and during the first two decades of U.S. jurisdiction over the Southwest they remained unconquered. A series of treaties was drawn up during this time and broken by both sides, and war broke out intermittently. Then Colonel Kit Carson headed a campaign to subdue the Navajos and finally succeeded in starving them into surrendering in 1864. Eight thousand Navajos—half the tribe—began the "Long Walk" to Fort Sumner, where they were confined for four years. Finally, under the Treaty of 1868, they were allowed to return to a portion of their homeland. Today there also

MASSIVE WALLS of Canyon de Chelly dwarf wagon of Navajo family. The dramatic Navajo country is the largest Indian reservation in the United States.

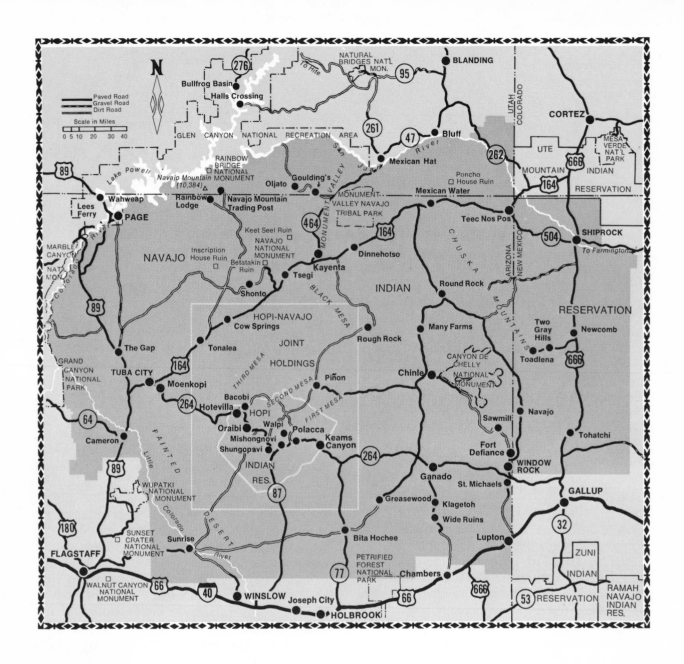

are three small Navajo reservations in New Mexico—Ramah, Cañoncito, and Alamo (see map on page 5), with a total population of about 3,000.

After the Fort Sumner captivity the Navajos rebuilt their economy on the basis of sheep and goats issued to them in 1869. Sheep-raising continues to be the most important single element in the Navajo economy, and almost all of the reservation is used as range land. But despite its vastness, the Navajo country has become overpopulated in terms of its ability to support a pastoral economy. By the mid 1940's, a study of reservation resources warned that not more than half the tribe could be supported by the arid land.

Fortunately, new sources of income have emerged. Uranium, oil, and gas discoveries have brought lease and royalty payments. The tribal council has taken steps to broaden the tribe's economic base, investing funds in job-creating enterprises—for instance, irrigation projects, a sawmill, and tourist facilities—and encouraging private corporations to establish plants on the reservation.

It was the discovery of oil on the reservation in the 1920's that eventually led to the formation of the Navajo Tribal Council. Previously not organized beyond family groups or local bands (this was what made the early treaties unrealistic—no single leader could sign a treaty on behalf of all the Navajos), the Navajos needed a central body authorized to negotiate leases. Today lively campaigns are conducted before tribal elections. A chairman, vice-chairman, and geographically representative 74-member council govern the tribe, and an annual budget of more than $15,000,000 is directed into such areas as housing programs, recreational development, and health and education facilities.

The Hopi Indians

The Hopis offer many contrasts to the Navajos who live all around them. Whereas the Navajos are recent arrivals in this part of the country, the Hopis are Shoshonean-speaking descendants of the ancient Anasazi city-builders who reached their cultural peak at such sites as Betatakin, Keet Seel, and Inscription House (see page 22) and left hundreds of village ruins scattered across the Southwest. Unlike the Navajos, the Hopis live almost entirely in villages; one of these settlements—Oraibi—is thought to have been occupied since 1150. The name "Hopi" comes from a word meaning "the peaceful people," and the Hopis were never at war with the United States.

Spanish explorers came to the Hopi mesas in the sixteenth century, and in 1629 Franciscan missionaries began establishing missions here. In 1680 the Hopis took part in the Pueblo Revolt (see page 39) and ejected the Spaniards. Reconquest of the pueblos did not extend to the Hopi villages, and life here is not the blend of Spanish-Christian and ancient Pueblo cultures that you find in the Rio Grande groups.

In 1848 the United States gained control of the region, and in 1882 the Hopi reservation was created. A tribal constitution was adopted in 1936 and the Hopi Tribal Council was recognized as the tribe's governing body in 1955, though not all of the villages participate in the council. Each village has its own leader, elective or hereditary.

Like their prehistoric ancestors, the Hopis are agriculturalists. Their fields of corn, beans, squash, and melons lie close to their villages, below the mesas. None of the farmland on the reservation is irrigated; only Moencopi, a Hopi town west of the reservation, has irrigated fields.

Ceremonies and special events

Dramatic religious ceremonies are conducted by both the Navajos and the Hopis, the most famous probably being the Hopi snake dance. Most of these ceremonies are scheduled only a short time ahead, and often seeing one of them is simply a matter of being in the right place at the right time. Traders and local residents may be able to give you information and directions. The Navajos also have several fairs and rodeos, and portions of various ceremonial dances often are performed at these. Other opportunities to observe costumed Indian dancers are at the Flagstaff Pow Wow (page 18), the Gallup Inter-Tribal Ceremonial (page 26), and the Bluff Indian Day (page 24).

Navajo ceremonies have to do with curing and usually involve a patient. Navajo medicine men or singers pass down the legends behind the rituals from one generation to another. One of the best known ceremonies is the Yei-be-chai, conducted only in winter and lasting for nine days.

BRILLIANTLY costumed butterfly maidens are among dancers at one of the impressive Hopi ceremonies.

On the last night the strangely costumed Yei-be-chais dance and sing in falsetto voices before a ceremonial hogan.

Navajo ceremonies begin late at night and last until dawn, and usually they are held at remote locations reached only by dirt trails.

Hopi religious rites take place in the village plazas and inside the ceremonial kivas, and the public may attend the part held in the plaza. Cameras and tape recorders are forbidden. From April through September there usually is at least one outdoor ceremony each weekend somewhere on the reservation.

The snake dance, a rain ceremony, usually takes place late in August. (To find out the exact date you can contact the Hopi Agency at Keams Canyon — 602-738-2225, through Holbrook — about the second week in August.) Hopis costumed in brightly decorated kilts and fox skins dance with live snakes—including rattlesnakes—held between their teeth. Hopis believe the snakes will carry messages to the rain gods, informing them of the need for rain. The snake dances are held at Shipaulovi, Shungopavi, and Hotevilla in even-numbered years and at Mishongnovi and Walpi in odd years. They generally start about 4 P.M. or later.

From January to late July the Hopi Kachina dances are held. Masked dancers representing various spirits accept petitions for rain, health, and good fortune and chastise those who have offended tribal law and custom. They also bring gifts of food to respected village elders and present *Kachintihii*—small effigies of Kachina spirits—to Hopi children. Unmasked dances are held from August to December.

Navajo and Hopi crafts

The Navajo's ability to take useful elements from other cultures and adapt them to his own way of life has always been one of his strengths. The Navajos learned the techniques of weaving from Pueblo Indians—perhaps ancestors of today's Hopis—and now are the best known Indian weavers. When the Spaniards brought sheep to the Southwest the Navajos began weaving with wool rather than cotton, and they produced fine blankets. Then commercially-made blankets became readily available in the late 1800's, and traders urged the Navajos to make the heavier rugs for which they are now best known. Weaving is a woman's occupation among the Navajos; in the Hopi villages, men are the weavers. Hopi men weave ceremonial robes and sashes.

From Mexican craftsmen the Navajos learned silversmithing in the mid-1800's. Coins were used for silver until this practice was prohibited; then the Indians obtained their silver through traders who got it from refineries. Navajos produce both hammered and sandcast jewelry (see page 45). Beginning in the late 1930's the Museum of Northern Arizona successfully undertook a program to encourage Hopi craftsmen to develop their own style of silverwork.

The Hopis are particularly known for their carved wooden Kachina dolls, which represent members of the Hopi spirit world. Hopi women produce good pottery—typically yellow-orange or reddish with black designs, a revival of styles from fourteenth-century pottery found by archeologists. Still another Hopi craft is basketry—both coiled and wicker. Hopi baskets are more colorful than those of many other Indian groups;

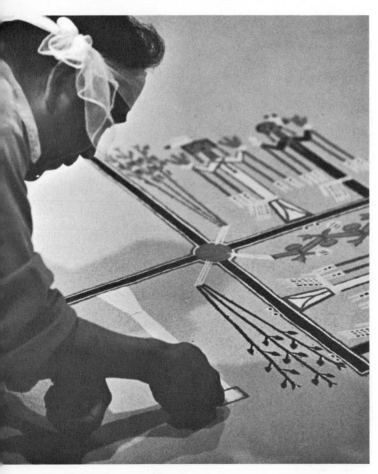

SAND-PAINTING process is part of Navajo religious ritual, sometimes can be seen at museum craft shows.

vegetable dyes are used as well as natural colors to make purple, blue, red, yellow, green, black.

Navajo sand painting is an art form, though its purpose is completely ceremonial. Curing ceremonies include the creation of a sand painting—more correctly called dry painting, since the materials are pollen, meal, crushed flowers, charcoal, and crushed minerals. The painting is destroyed after the religious ritual.

Both the Navajos and the Hopis have formed craft guilds. The Navajo Arts and Crafts Guild is a tribal enterprise which was started in 1941 to promote quality workmanship and better earnings for craftsmen. The guild's headquarters are at Window Rock, and there are branches at Tuba City, Navajo National Monument, Monument Valley, Kayenta, Teec Nos Pos, Chinle, and Cameron. On the Hopi reservation, both the Hopi Arts and Crafts-Silvercrafts Cooperative on Second Mesa and Hopi Enterprises on Third Mesa

are cooperative organizations. You also can find Navajo and Hopi work of excellent quality at many trading posts on the reservations and at shops in off-reservation cities.

Special sightseeing tours

There are a number of ways of traveling through this part of Indian country. Besides driving yourself, you can take one of the reservation tours recently started by the Navajo tribe. For an overview, take a plane or helicopter tour. And to reach some back-country places you must travel in a four-wheel-drive vehicle, on horesback, in a boat—or on foot.

The five-day package tours offered by the Navajos take you to the Window Rock area, Monument Valley, Navajo National Monument, Lake Powell, Canyon de Chelly, and Hubbell Trading Post. Navajo college students are your guides,

THE GEOGRAPHY OF NAVAJO RUGS

A Navajo weaver carries the entire pattern for a rug in her head as she works, and no design is ever repeated exactly. Still, some general pattern types prevail, and a connoisseur can tell where most rugs come from.

Black, white, gray, and brown are natural wool colors. Aniline dyes account for the brilliant reds, blues, and other bright colors in some rugs. Painstakingly brewed vegetable dyes, a more recent development, produce wonderfully soft colors; dealers often have charts showing the plants that produce these dyes.

These are some of the centers of Navajo weaving and the styles most typical of them:

• Tuba City area is known for "storm pattern" rugs, designed with a center box shape connected by lightning symbols to smaller squares in the corners. Black, white, gray, and red are the most common, but you can find storm patterns in other colors as well.

• Teec Nos Pos, near the Four Corners, is the center for the outline rug, in which geometric shapes in the design are outlined in another color. Often many bright aniline-dye colors are woven into a single rug.

• Shiprock region produces most of the *yei*

blankets—the design consists of narrow, elongated figures representing supernatural beings. The rugs themselves do not have any religious significance, however. Yei blankets most often have a white background. They are popular as wall hangings.

• Two Gray Hills is famous for its expertly woven rugs of finely spun yarn. Intricate geometric designs are executed in natural wool colors; often there is a black border.

• Crystal, north of Window Rock, uses vegetable dyes in brown, yellow, rust, green, and black. The simple design is in bands, sometimes in wavy lines.

• Wide Ruins-Pine Springs, near the reservation's southeastern corner, produces some outstanding examples of vegetable-dye rugs in soft shades along with some designs in natural colors.

• Ganado area is best known for its rugs of red, black, gray, and white geometric designs; the dark red used in these rugs has become known as "Ganado red." Today vegetable dyes also are used here.

• Keams Canyon rugs are typically red, black, gray, and white like those of Ganado, but one distinguishing feature of some is their large size —up to 15 by 30 feet.

and travel is in buses carrying seven to twelve passengers (each tour is kept to 30 persons or less). Tours are conducted from April through November, starting on Mondays, Wednesdays, and Fridays. For more information, write to the Navajo Parks and Recreation Department, Window Rock, Arizona 86515.

Aerial tours can take you in only an hour or two over remote sights that would take you many hours to reach on the ground. For information, check at any airport with commercial services in the region.

Four-wheel-drive tours are available in many primitive scenic areas, such as Monument Valley and Canyon de Chelly. Horse or mule trips go to some places that even four-wheel-drive vehicles can't take you. Sightseeing from the waterways includes float trips down the Colorado River and motorboat excursions on Lake Powell.

Hunting and fishing

Big game can be hunted on the Navajo reservation in season, set each fall by the tribal council. Predators, rabbits, and squirrels can also be hunted. You can obtain hunting permits at Fish and Wildlife offices in Window Rock and in cities near the reservation and at certain trading posts.

All lakes and streams on the Navajo reservation have a year-round fishing season; you must have a tribal permit in addition to a state license. The Chuska Mountains in the eastern part of the reservation have numerous lakes and streams where you can fish for trout, catfish, and bluegill, and there is good wintertime ice fishing at Wheatfields, Tsaile, and Little Whitecone lakes in this region. Giant Lake Powell, at the reservation's northern edge, has been stocked with rainbow trout, largemouth bass, and Kokanee salmon.

For further information, contact the Fish and Wildlife Section, Parks and Recreation Department, Box 155, Window Rock, Arizona 86515.

Camping

The Navajo tribe has built nearly 50 campgrounds on its reservation (no camping permit required), and many of the national park service areas on and near the reservation also have campgrounds. You may camp at several sites on the Hopi reservation.

THE FLAGSTAFF AREA

The city of Flagstaff, located just beyond the southwest corner of the Navajo Indian Reservation, is one of the gateways to the reservation. For the traveler interested in Indian history and crafts, Flagstaff itself has much to offer. The Museum of Northern Arizona has fine exhibits on both Indian arts and history and the geology of the area. Nearby are the ruins of ancient Indian villages. And if you are in Flagstaff over the Fourth of July weekend, you can attend the happy-go-lucky, loosely organized spectacular known as the All-Indian Pow Wow.

For many northern Arizona tribes, the pow wow is a two or three-generation tradition. Its schedule is flexible. The parade gets started down Santa Fe Avenue *about* 11 A.M. each day; the rodeo takes place each afternoon *around* 1:30; and the ceremonials begin nightly at 8—or thereabouts. Reserved seats at the night ceremonials are $3 each; general admission (on sale an hour ahead) is $2 for adults, $1 for children under 12. Prices are the same for the afternoon rodeo.

Out at the encampment, the pickup camper has almost replaced the wagon and tepee, but visitors are very much aware that they are touring a real Indian camp. Ponies are hobbled amongst the confusion of cars, trucks, tents, and wagons; freshly butchered sheep hang from the tree branches. Along the outer fringe of the encampment, craftsmen throw together crude lean-tos to display rugs, pottery, basketry, and jewelry.

Museum of Northern Arizona

Extensive exhibits of Indian arts and crafts are displayed at the Museum of Northern Arizona, and at special museum crafts shows you can see Indian artists at work. The museum's stone buildings are set in a pine forest 3 miles north of downtown Flagstaff via U.S. Highway 180.

Three exhibit rooms contain carving, metalworking, weaving, pottery, and musical instruments made by Indian craftsmen—mainly Hopis and Navajos. One large room is devoted entirely to a display of Navajo rugs, tracing the history of their weaving with examples of each major type.

The museum's three remaining exhibit rooms offer a comprehensive and easy-to-understand geological survey of northern Arizona.

During the Fourth of July weekend the museum stages a Hopi art show. Pottery, baskets, sil-

THE BEST of Hopi craftwork is on display during annual Hopi art show at the Museum of Northern Arizona.

FLAGSTAFF POW WOW is a time of reunion for many tribes. Indian encampment set up during festivities is crowded with wagons and ponies, and the air is sweet with smell of cedar smoke.

ver jewelry, sashes, and blankets are displayed, and Hopi craftsmen demonstrate how they are made. A woodcarver creates brightly-colored Kachina dolls against the backdrop of the museum's own Kachina collection. Crafts displayed are for sale, but since only the finest examples are exhibited, the shopping is pretty much limited to serious collectors. For just 15 cents, however, you can buy a roll of thinly layered blue cornmeal piki bread, hot from a stone griddle.

Late in July the finest examples of Navajo work are assembled for the museum's week-long Navajo Craftsmen Exhibition. Rugs and silverwork are featured, and each day of the show you can see a weaver working at a crude handmade loom and a silversmith creating silver and turquoise jewelry. The crafts on exhibit are offered for sale.

Walnut Canyon National Monument

Nine hundred years ago a volcano eruption near present-day Flagstaff had a major effect on Indian life in the area. Walnut Canyon National Monument is part of that story, as are nearby Sunset Crater and Wupatki national monuments. To reach Walnut Canyon, drive east from Flagstaff for 7 miles on U.S. Highway 66-Interstate 40 to the monument entrance, turn right, and continue another 3 miles to the visitor center.

Because the volcanic eruption turned an 800-square-mile area into rich farmland, a number of different Indian groups migrated to this region. Some of the Sinagua Indians who had already lived here were crowded out and moved to the snaking canyon of now-dry Walnut Creek, south of the volcano. Applying masonry skills learned from pueblo builders who had moved into the area, they walled up cavelike recesses in the limestone walls of the 400-foot-deep canyon. The remains of more than 300 small cliff rooms are preserved in Walnut Canyon National Monument.

A level 5/8-mile trail along the canyon rim provides overlooks of the ruins, and close-up views of two surface dwellings. A more strenuous 3/4-mile hike leads past ruins constructed on the sides of a steep rocky peninsula, descending 185 feet into the canyon before leveling out for a loop walk past about 25 cliffside rooms; the round trip takes about 40 minutes.

Walnut Canyon is open daily from 7 A.M. to 7 P.M. from Memorial Day to Labor Day, 8 A.M. to 5 P.M. the rest of the year. Admission is $1 per car.

Sunset Crater and Wupatki National Monuments

Arizona's first real estate boom occurred some 900 years ago on the high plateau that stretches from the San Francisco Peaks to the canyon of the Little Colorado. In 1065 a great eruption of the volcano now called Sunset Crater spread a thick covering of cinder and ash across the arid plateau, forming an excellent mulch. Soon Indians were migrating from less favored areas to farm the rich land, and the area became a cultural melting pot. You can visit the volcanic crater and the ruins of the Indians' villages at two national monuments joined by a paved loop from U.S. Highway 89.

The side road to Sunset Crater swings eastward from the highway about 15 miles northeast of Flagstaff, and the visitor center is 4 miles beyond. There is an exhibit of the area's volcanic history here and a 45-unit campground across the road. You can circle a section of the lava field in a 45-minute walk along Lava Flow Trail; at one point you'll come to an ice cave several hundred feet long. If you're willing and able to undertake a strenuous hour's hike, climb the 1,000 feet to the crater rim (sturdy hiking boots are advisable); from the summit you see the Painted Desert and the mesas of the Hopi and Navajo reservations. Sunset Crater is open daily from 7 A.M. to 7 P.M. in summer, 8 A.M. to 5 P.M. in winter. There is no admission fee.

About 15 miles farther on the loop road is the visitor center of Wupatki National Monument, site of 800 known Indian ruins. Wupatki ruin itself—Hopi for "tall house"—is the most completely excavated; it once housed some 200 people in more than 100 rooms. You can explore this four-story dwelling in an hour or less. On the way out to U.S. 89 (14 miles from the visitor center) you pass other ruins, including the Citadel—unexcavated but well worth a visit for its impressive size and commanding view of the surrounding area.

Wupatki visitor center is open daily except Christmas and Thanksgiving from 8 A.M. to 7 P.M. in summer, 8 A.M. to 5 P.M. in winter. Admission is free.

NORTHEAST ON U.S. 164

North of Flagstaff on U.S. 89 you enter the Navajo Indian Reservation. Soon you will see a colorful landscape called the Painted Desert; its best known section lies to the east, just north of U.S. Highway 66 near Petrified Forest National Park.

At its junction with U.S. 89, head east on U.S. Highway 164 to Tuba City. From there the highway angles north and brings you close to the most impressive prehistoric pueblo dwellings on the reservation and then to the colorful silhouettes of Monument Valley.

Tuba City and a Hopi town

The principal community on the western part of the Navajo reservation is Tuba City, known to the Navajos as Tonanesdizi—"tangled water"— because of the springs that feed several reservoirs in the area.

Tuba City is about 10 miles east of U.S. 89 on U.S. Highway 164. About 5 miles before you reach town you can make a short side trip to see evidences of dinosaurs that walked over the mud flats of northern Arizona around 180 million years ago. The ancient mud upon which they left their footprints was gradually covered with more mud which in time hardened into rock, but centuries of erosion have uncovered some of the tracks. About 500 feet up a clearly marked gravel road leading off the highway you will find the prints, just opposite a small, waterless picnic area. There also is a small reservoir about 3 miles up this road; take the left fork. In the vicinity are several Navajo hogans.

In Tuba City there are such modern buildings as a community center, a hospital, schools, and a supermarket. The Navajo Tribal Ranger in Tuba City can tell you about points of interest, several campgrounds in the area, and reservoirs where you may fish. Tuba City is the site of a Navajo fair in October.

Two miles southeast of Tuba City is a Hopi farming settlement called Moenkopi, established long before the creation of the Hopi reservation to the east. Navajos and Hopis work together in Tuba City while still maintaining their separate languages and traditions, and the Hopi houses of stone and mud plaster are very different from the Navajo hogans.

Navajo National Monument

Long before the Navajos established themselves in the area a branch of the pueblo-dwelling

Anasazi people lived in several cliff dwellings west of Kayenta. The three well preserved ruins known as Navajo National Monument represent the peak of their cultural achievements. To explore these back-country ruins and nearby trading posts, drive 50 miles northeast from Tuba City on U.S. Highway 164 to a paved 9-mile road that branches north to monument headquarters.

Start your exploring at the headquarters, situated on the rim of red-walled Tsegi Canyon. Excellent exhibits will introduce you to the ancient

BETATAKIN was built in arch of huge cave, is most accessible of Navajo National Monument ruins.

MONUMENT VALLEY skyline is backdrop for Navajo sheepherders moving herd to new grazing area. Spire at right center is Totem Pole; to left is Yei Bichei, named for line of dancers in Navajo ceremony.

culture of the Kayenta Anasazi, a branch of the same people that built cities at Mesa Verde and Chaco Canyon (see page 52), then suddenly moved on. The Kayenta people probably moved only a few miles south, where the Hopi towns are inhabited by their descendants.

Navajo National Monument's three cliff ruins are Betatakin, Keet Seel, and Inscription House, built in the latter part of the 1200's and abandoned about 1300. Betatakin was built at the mouth of a huge cave; you can see it from the opposite wall of the canyon by following Sandal Trail from headquarters to a viewing terrace on the canyon rim. The round-trip walk takes from 40 minutes to an hour.

If you'd like to climb down the canyon wall along a stone stairway for a closer look at Betatakin's 135 rooms, you must go with a park ranger. Tours are conducted at 8:30 A.M. and 1:30 P.M., and each lasts about three hours. Going down is difficult and coming up is exhausting, but the ruins and the lovely, aspen-filled canyon bottom are worth the trip if you are in fair condition.

Keet Seel—the largest cliff dwelling in Arizona —and Inscription House are much more difficult to visit. Horses can be rented for a guided, all-day trip to Keet Seel and back (16 miles in all); notify the monument superintendent the day before you want to make this trip. Inscription House, 30 miles from monument headquarters, is reached by a 5-mile round-trip hike. Ask the rangers for directions to these sites, and be sure to register at headquarters when you leave and return.

Navajo shepherds have occupied the monument area for the last hundred years, and behind the headquarters building you will find an old-style hogan and a tiny Navajo bathhouse. The Navajo Arts and Crafts Guild outlet at the visitor center offers a selection of rugs and jewelry. A 28-unit campground is located nearby.

A back road from the monument leads 10 miles southwest to an interesting trading post at Shonto; another trading post is Tsegi, on the highway 7 miles northeast of the turnoff to the monument.

A primitive road leads north of Navajo National Monument to Navajo Mountain Trading Post and Rainbow Lodge, from where you can hike or ride horseback to Rainbow Bridge National Monument (see page 33 for information about the water route to Rainbow Bridge). Inquire about road conditions before starting.

Monument Valley

The famed buttes and spires of Monument Valley can be glimpsed from the highway, but to

enjoy the full impact of this incomparable landscape along the Utah-Arizona border you must take time to leave the main roads. At Monument Valley Navajo Tribal Park you can take in a wide view of the valley from a glass-walled observatory, and you can drive into the park in your own car on a 16-mile loop road. If you have time for more exploring, you can arrange for a guided tour in a four-wheel-drive vehicle that will take you to areas inaccessible by passenger car.

To reach the tribal park headquarters, turn east from Utah Highway 47 (Arizona Highway 464 until it crosses the state border) a half-mile north of the state line. (To the west this road leads to the Monument Valley Seventh-Day Adventist Hospital and to Goulding's Trading Post and Lodge.) The visitor center at the park entrance is 4 miles from the highway. Besides the observatory, the visitor center contains a Navajo Arts and Crafts Guild display room. An adjacent campground has 15 sites.

Navajo Tribal Rangers will collect a fee of 75 cents per person (children under 12 free) if you wish to drive into the park. Personnel are on duty at the park from 8 A.M. to 5 P.M. daily in winter, 7 A.M. to 7 P.M. daily in summer.

Monument Valley is the home of Navajos today, and you are likely to see a Navajo weaver with her loom set up outdoors. In prehistoric

INDIAN PICTURE-WRITING

Although pictographs are defined as all human communication by means of pictures, the word usually refers to primitive rock paintings. Petroglyphs, on the other hand, refer to incised, pecked, or abraded pictures on rocks. Often incised drawings are painted afterward.

As a forerunner of writing, ideographic drawings conveyed ideas directly. For example, on a precipitous trail in New Mexico, a symbol for "no thoroughfare" was found in a nearby rock drawing. The picture showed a mountain goat standing upright and a horse and rider upside down, warning that the trail may be easy enough for goats, but not for horses and riders.

Petroglyphs were made by pecking simple, linear figures out of smooth vertical rocks using hammerstones. Pictographs (also known as petrograms) were made by using natural dyes—iron oxides, mercury, lime, and manganese—to make red, yellow, white, orange, and black.

Pictographs and petroglyphs are found throughout the Southwest. At an early period, Pueblo groups developed an abstract style which can be seen today in their textiles, pottery, and costumes. They used many colors. In eastern Arizona and Utah, realistic or naturalistic figures predominated.

times, too, Indians lived here, as you will see from their ancient pictographs, petroglyphs, and ruins.

For information about all-day commercial tours of the back country, inquire at the tribal ranger station or contact Canyon Country Scenic Tours, Mexican Hat, Utah 84531; Golden Sands Tours, Kayenta, Arizona 86033; Goulding's Monument Valley Tours, Monument Valley, Utah 84536; or Tours of the Big Country, Bluff, Utah 84512.

Overnight accommodations are available in Kayenta, Mexican Hat, and Monument Valley.

UTAH'S CANYON COUNTRY

From Monument Valley you can either return to Kayenta or continue northeast into the canyon country of Utah's southeast corner. You cross the San Juan River and leave the Navajo reservation at Mexican Hat, named for a balanced rock which

PONCHO HOUSE is a major Anasazi cliff ruin on Navajo reservation in Utah canyon country. Jeep tours come here from Mexican Hat, Bluff.

reminded settlers of an upside-down sombrero. Until quite recently the town was a thriving uranium camp. From Mexican Hat, a 10-mile drive leads west to an overlook of the spectacular Goosenecks of the San Juan, a series of tortuous meanders of the San Juan canyon; take the turn-off from State Highway 261 left to Goosenecks State Park.

Bluff

The quiet little town of Bluff, about 36 miles northeast of Mexican Hat on State 47, is a trading center for Navajo and Ute Indians and the site of an all-tribes Indian Day in June and an Indian rodeo on July 4. The town includes a primary school, a cafe, a rock shop, and a couple of motels, and beyond its eastern margins is St. Christopher's Mission to the Navajo. Not far from the mission are the ruins of a thirteenth century cliff dwelling.

Indian Day is regularly scheduled for the third Saturday in June. The program is quite informal and is likely to include Indian dances, pony races, frybread contests, and intertribal tugs-of-war. Admission is $1 for adults, 50 cents for children under 12.

The church building of St. Christopher's, an Episcopal mission, is an impressive pyramid of cedar shakes and glass. Staff members will show you around the mission and explain its programs. A small trading post at the mission sells Indian crafts. From St. Christopher's, an improved road heads east for about a mile to a swaying footbridge that crosses the San Juan River to the Navajo reservation. You can leave your car by the bridge and walk across the river to a trail that leads to a cliff dwelling abandoned in the late 1200's. A group of pictographs can be seen on the canyon wall.

For escorted tours of the mission or for information on four-wheel-drive vehicle tours and river trips, inquire at Recapture Lodge in Bluff.

Natural Bridges and Glen Canyon

Utah's canyon country once was part of an inland sea. As the sea retreated, wind and water began to strip away the thick layers of sediment that had accumulated over 500 million years, cutting deep canyons and exposing the volcanic roots of mountains. Some of the dramatic results

MUSCLES STRAIN as Ute Indians (in foreground) challenge Navajos to an intertribal tug-of-war during the annual Indian Day festivities at Bluff. Other activities include dances, pony races.

of this erosion can be seen at lookouts accessible by car, but you must travel by four-wheel-drive vehicle, horse, airplane, or boat for more extensive exploring.

Natural Bridges National Monument encompasses three stone bridges formed over a period of centuries by the force of streams hitting against the rocks. You reach the monument by state highways 261 and 95 from Mexican Hat or by State 95 from Blanding. A 9-mile paved loop road takes you to viewpoints overlooking Sipapu, Kachina, and Owachomo bridges. Each is accessible over a short trail. Sipapu is the highest of the three at 200 feet and has the greatest span—268 feet. Also within the monument boundaries are about 200 small ruins left by Indians who lived here from about 2,000 to 650 years ago. If you hike to the bridges you will see one cliff dwelling of about 20 rooms, several small rooms on high ledges, and a kiva with the original roof and ladder intact. To enter any ruin site you must obtain permission from the park ranger at the visitor center.

West of Natural Bridges you can reach Lake Powell in Glen Canyon National Recreation Area on either State 95 to Hite or another dirt road branching southwest to Halls Crossing. At Halls Crossing there are rental boats, excursions, launching facilities, boating and camping supplies, trailer hookups, and a primitive campground. A ranger is on duty in the summer. Hite has boat-fuel service, limited camping supplies, and some primitive camping sites. Bullfrog Basin, reached by paved highway on the west side of the lake, has launching facilities, boat rentals, a campground, and a store.

SOUTH FROM THE FOUR CORNERS

At only one spot in the United States can you touch the ground of four different states at once. The Four Corners Monument marks the place where Utah, Colorado, New Mexico, and Arizona meet. To reach it, drive east on U.S. 164 from Kayenta; take the left branch at Teec Nos Pos, where the road forks, and take the turnoff to the Four Corners Monument.

Then return to Teec Nos Pos and turn left for Shiprock, New Mexico, the principal community in the northeastern part of the reservation. To the right of the road you will spot the towering stone formation that gives the town its name; it dominates the skyline for miles. Shiprock is the center of a farming belt irrigated by water from the San Juan and the site of a popular district fair in September. The Navajo tribe operates a restaurant and a motel (Nataani Nez Lodge) here.

About 18 miles to the east, near Fruitland but on the south side of the river, is the Four Corners Power Plant, with the strip-mine coal deposits that fuel it and the lake created to provide water for its steam generators. The reservoir, Lake Morgan, is open to recreational use.

South of Shiprock is an area famed for the high quality of its weaving. Just beyond Newcomb, turn southwest on U.S. Highway 666 onto the gravel road leading to the Two Gray Hills and Toadlena trading posts. For years, Two Gray Hills rugs have been leading entries at the tribal fair and at Indian crafts exhibits elsewhere.

Back on the highway, you drive along the east side of the pine-forested Chuska Mountains and around the southern end of the range. You can either continue south for a side trip to Gallup or turn west on State Highway 264 to reach the Navajo capital of Window Rock.

Gallup and the Inter-Tribal Ceremonial

One of the Southwest's most colorful Indian celebrations is the Inter-Tribal Ceremonial presented in Gallup each year for four days in mid-August. About 30 different tribes participate in an Indian rodeo, parades (tribal groups in costume, Indian bands, horsemen), dances, and displays (all craft articles are for sale).

During the Gallup festivities you are likely to see Totanac dancers from Mexico performing atop an 85-foot-high pole, Zuni maidens marching with pottery *ollas* (water jugs) balanced on their heads, and Yakima chiefs in tribal finery riding palomino horses. For information and tickets, write to the Inter-Tribal Indian Ceremonial Association, Box 1029, Gallup, New Mexico 87301. Prices for adults range from $2 to $7.50, reserved seats, and $1 to $2.50, general admission; lower rates are charged for children under 13.

Plans are underway to expand the Gallup ceremonial into a year-around American Indian Park and Cultural Center with an amphitheatre for ceremonial programs, an arts and crafts center, a plaza for craft demonstrations, an Indian village, and a museum. This complex is to be located 7 miles east of downtown Gallup along Interstate 40.

FROM THE CAPITAL TO THE CANYON

A section of the Navajo reservation in the far eastern part of Arizona includes both some of the tribe's most progressive developments and some of its most interesting historical sites. From the reservation's hub city of Window Rock you head west on State Highway 264, and just beyond an old-time trading post you turn north for the drive to colorful Canyon de Chelly.

Window Rock, the Navajo capital

The affairs of the largest Indian tribe in the country are directed from the sandstone buildings near the weather-carved rock formation that gives Window Rock its name. Nearby are a tribal museum, the headquarters of the crafts guild, and the fairgrounds where Navajos assemble for the annual tribal fair.

Window Rock is located just inside the Arizona border; you turn north onto a paved road from State 264 just after you cross the state line from the east and re-enter the reservation. North of the junction are the capitol buildings—the octagonal chamber of the tribal council and offices of the tribal organization and the government's Navajo Agency. The interior of the council chamber is decorated with murals of scenes from Navajo history; the building usually is open to the public, and you may attend meetings of the council. The capitol buildings are clustered among smoothed sandstone hills called the Haystacks, and overlooking them is the hole-in-the-rock landmark that is now part of Window Rock Tribal Park.

Back at the junction, the guild display rooms are worthy of some browsing time. The craftwork here is among the Navajos' finest. The showrooms are open from 8 A.M. to 5 P.M. (6 P.M. in summer) Monday through Friday, 9 A.M. to 5 P.M. Saturday, and 1 to 4 P.M. Sunday.

Just up the road are the fairgrounds, visitor center (free brochures and maps are available here), civic center, and tribal museum. The museum has exhibits devoted to Navajo crafts, religion, and history; ancient cultures; and geology and plant and animal life of the reservation. In back of the museum is a zoo with many of the birds and mammals native to the reservation. The museum is open daily from 8 A.M. to 5 P.M.; admission is free.

TRIBAL FAIR annually brings kaleidoscope of color and activity to Window Rock, the Navajo capital.

WEATHER-CARVED formation gave community of Window Rock its name, is now part of a tribal park.

The fairgrounds area, with its circular civic center building, exhibit halls, rodeo arena and grandstand, is the focal point of activity for thousands of Indians who are drawn to Window Rock early in September for the four-day Navajo Tribal Fair. Conventional modern dress mingles with bright calico and velveteen, and over the public address system announcements are made in Navajo, then in English. You can divide your time between scheduled events (such as a rodeo, ceremonial dances, concerts by the tribal band, and a queen contest) and visits to the exhibit halls (ribbon-winning rugs and jewelry, produce, and livestock plus displays explaining services of the tribal organization). Outside is the midway, complete with rides, games of skill, and refreshment stands—some of which offer such Navajo specialties as frybread. One very popular fair event is a free barbecue.

The fairgrounds are also the site of a three-day rodeo—Ahoo'hai Days—held each year over the Fourth of July.

There are overnight accommodations in Window Rock (including the tribally operated Window Rock Lodge), but to stay here during the fair you must make reservations well ahead. An improved campground at Window Rock Tribal Park fills up early, too. Seven miles west of Window Rock on State 264 is Summit Campground, set among ponderosa pines.

Three nearby communities

Near Window Rock are the communities of Fort Defiance, Navajo, and St. Michaels—the first permanent U.S. Army post in Navajo country, a lumber town, and a Franciscan mission.

Fort Defiance, 6 miles north of Window Rock, was established in 1851 as an outpost in the military actions against the Navajos. Later it was Kit Carson's headquarters during the last Navajo campaign. The government's first Navajo Agency was located here from 1868 until 1936.

Farther north (15 miles from Window Rock) and on the other side of Black Creek is the community of Navajo, designed from the ground up by a San Francisco planning firm. The nearby

SPIDER ROCK *soars 800 feet high, marks place where Canyon de Chelly meets Monument Valley. At right, rooms tucked in mineral-streaked cliff are among hundreds of ruins in canyon complex.*

HOGAN *of mud and stone is Navajo farmhouse, belies seeming emptiness of quiet canyon floor.*

tribal sawmill employs about 500 Navajos and is the reason the town was built. Two miles west of Window Rock (just south of State 264) is St. Michael's, where the Franciscans founded a mission school late in the 1890's. St. Michael's is the largest mission school on the reservation.

Ganado and Hubbell Trading Post

Drive west on State 264 to Ganado to visit a trading post reminiscent of the early days of Indian traders on the reservation. At Ganado you also can tour the 200-acre campus of Ganado Presbyterian Mission, and farther east you can see prehistoric ruins at a Navajo tribal park.

Horsecollars and cradleboards hang alongside shelves of canned goods and bolts of yardage at the Hubbell Trading Post, a short detour off State 264 just past Ganado. Since Lorenzo Hubbell founded the trading post in 1876 the Indians have come here to trade their wool, rugs, and jewelry for coffee, saddles, and other supplies. Here also they visit with old friends, gossip about tribal affairs, and discuss sheep, grazing lands, and rain.

Since 1967 the trading post, the old Hubbell home, and the barn have been a national historic site, but business continues as usual under the management of the Southwestern Monuments Association. Perhaps while you are at the trading post you will see the trader weigh a big sackful of piñon nuts to buy from the Navajo who gathered them, or return a beautiful silver and turquoise necklace consigned to the pawn closet when the owner needed cash.

Guided tours of the trading post (including rooms stocked with Navajo rugs and silver jewelry) and the Hubbell home are available daily from 8 A.M. until 4 P.M.; the site is open until 5 P.M., later during the summer. In the home are many mementoes of reservation life and a fascinating collection of paintings. In the main room be sure to look up—beautifully woven baskets line the ceiling.

About a mile west of Hubbell Trading Post is Ganado Mission, a splash of green against the tan and pink of the surrounding rangeland. The mission church, a high school, and Sage Memorial Hospital (presently operated by Project Hope) are among the 60 buildings on the shaded campus. A hostess conducts tours. The mission has been in operation since 1901.

Eight miles east of Ganado is the turnoff to Kinlichee Tribal Park, 640 acres encompassing Anasazi ruins occupied between 800 and 1300 A.D. To reach the park you drive over a dirt road for 2½ miles north of Cross Canyon Trading Post. A self-guiding trail takes you past the ruins, one of which has been completely reconstructed. A shaded picnic area overlooks the site.

Canyon de Chelly National Monument

The Navajos call it *Tsegi*, "the Canyon." For more than 300 years its fortresslike walls, rising to heights of more than a thousand feet, have been a sanctuary for them. Today Canyon de Chelly is a living museum of a way of life that has almost vanished from the rest of the vast Navajo reservation.

Since 1931, through a lease agreement with the Navajo tribe, about 130 square miles of the Canyon de Chelly-Canyon del Muerto complex have been administered as a national monument. To reach it, follow a paved highway north from State 264 about 6 miles west of Ganado. After 30 miles, take the right fork, drive through Chinle, and continue to the Canyon de Chelly National Monument headquarters.

The Spanish were the first unsuccessful invaders of Canyon de Chelly (pronounced "de SHAY"). They came to punish the marauders who had repeatedly raided the villages of New Spain. But the Navajos simply withdrew into the vast labyrinth. U.S. Cavalry forces tried for almost 20 years to succeed where the Spanish had failed, but Canyon de Chelly remained impregnable. Then late in 1863 an expeditionary force under the command of Kit Carson burned crops, destroyed orchards, and slaughtered livestock. Starvation accomplished what no invading army had been able to do; bands of weary Navajos began to straggle into Fort Defiance. That spring the conquered people were herded like cattle across 300 miles of mountain and desert to confinement near Fort Sumner. Four years later, they were allowed to return.

Today the stubbornly preserved tribal heritage often is lost in the complexities of modern life, but some 400 Navajos who prefer the old ways return to Canyon de Chelly each spring to plant their crops, tend their orchards, and graze their sheep in the quiet manner of their forefathers. The canyon may seem as deserted as the ancient cliff dwellings that stand against its sandstone walls, but the smoke of a cooking fire drifting up from a lonely hogan gives occasional proof that this peaceful place is populated.

Though the Navajos consider the canyon their ancestral homeland, they were preceded by Anasazi people who built houses in open caves along the canyon walls and beneath overhanging ledges on the canyon floor. Most of the larger ruins were built between 1100 and 1200 A.D., culminating with the sophisticated square tower construction in Mummy Cave near the head of Canyon del Muerto. About 1300 the Anasazi abandoned the canyon, apparently because of prolonged drought and increasing raids by what may have been the forerunners of the present-day Navajos and Apaches.

Visitors can drive along the south rim of the canyon to five spectacular overlooks but are not allowed within the canyons unless accompanied by an authorized guide—the one exception is a mile-long trail from the canyon rim down to White House Ruin. Half-day and all-day canyon tours in four-wheel-drive vehicles are available at Justin's Thunderbird Lodge near the mouth of Canyon de Chelly. Accommodations are available here and in Chinle, and there is a 92-unit campground at the canyon mouth.

THE BEAT of a drum and the sound of ceremonial chants fill the Hopi villages during religious dances.

Saddle horses can be rented from a park concessionaire from mid-May to mid-September, and there are all-day guided horseback trips to White House Ruin. Park rangers conduct hikes into the canyons from monument headquarters each day and present evening campfire lectures in the public campground during the summer; inquire at the monument headquarters for the day's program. A museum here offers good exhibits on the history of the canyon.

Many Farms

Before returning to State 264 and heading west to the Hopi mesas, you can drive 14 miles north from Chinle to Many Farms to see one of the reservation's many irrigation projects. To the west is the long, imposing skyline of Black Mesa.

Navaho Community College is sharing the campus of Many Farms High School until construction is completed at its permanent site (scheduled for 1971) at Tsaile Lake, just northeast of Canyon de Chelly National Monument. The Navajo-run college opened in January of 1969 and now has about 500 students. Navajo cultural studies are stressed.

THE HOPI MESAS

The pueblo villages of the Hopis are situated on or near three mesas within the Hopi Indian Reservation. State 264 crosses the reservation and passes close to most of the villages, though there are no paved roads leading directly to them. A few miles after you enter the reservation you reach Keams Canyon, the site of the government Hopi Agency but not an Indian village. Most of the buildings in Keams Canyon (including the agency office, a hospital, and a boarding school) are government owned.

From Keams Canyon the highway takes you to the three mesas. First Mesa's villages are Walpi (the most picturesquely located), Sichomovi, and Hano (built by Tewa-speaking Indians from the Rio Grande after the 1680 Pueblo Revolt), with Polacca below at the base. On twin-pronged Second Mesa are Shungopavi, Shipaulovi, and Mishongnovi, and Toreva is below the mesa. The villages of the Third Mesa are Hotevilla, Bacobi, and ancient Oraibi; New Oraibi is situated at the base of the mesa overlooking Oraibi Wash.

Oraibi vies with Acoma pueblo in New Mexico

HOPI PUEBLOS are atop three mesas. At left, children play among crumbling walls at the Third Mesa village of Oraibi, one of oldest settlements in country. Walpi, right, is at tip of First Mesa.

(see page 42) for the distinction of being the oldest continuously-inhabited settlement in the United States. It probably has been occupied since about 1150, and until 1906 it was the largest Hopi town. Then many of its most conservative residents moved away and established Hotevilla. Other people from Oraibi have moved to New Oraibi. Tribal headquarters are at New Oraibi.

Village pageantry

The Hopi towns are treeless, sun-baked, and wind-swept, but their drabness is transformed by brilliant ceremonial pageantry that takes place in the village plazas. The most conclusive evidence that a dance is underway may be a concentration of cars and pickup trucks around one of the villages. Indian police or village authorities usually are on hand to direct parking. As you approach the plaza you may hear the muffled cadence of a drum, then a chorus of voices singing plaintively.

The plaza is crowded with Hopis wearing their finest jewelry and sashes. Ceremonial leaders and village elders often are seated in places of honor at the edge of the plaza, while youngsters take advantage of the better view from the rooftops. If the dance is a Kachina ceremony, the masked

impersonators interrupt the precision ritual at regular intervals to distribute gifts—three-lobed loaves of Pueblo bread still warm from the ovens, pumpkin pies, and even canned goods and sacks of flour from the trading post.

Shops and accommodations

Another reason for visiting the Hopi reservation is to see the fine pottery, baskets, silver jewelry, and carved Kachina dolls that the Hopis make. High quality crafts are sold at the Hopi Arts and Crafts-Silvercrafts Cooperative Guild on Second Mesa (at Piñon junction), at Hopi Enterprises in New Oraibi, and at trading posts in New Oraibi, Second Mesa, Polacca, and Hotevilla. Pottery is made in the First Mesa villages, coil basketry on Second Mesa, and wicker baskets on Third Mesa.

Overnight accommodations are limited to a motel at Keams Canyon; there are cafes in Keams Canyon and New Oraibi. You can camp at Keams Canyon Public Park for $1 per night, and overnight trailer parking facilities are available at Hopi Tribal Trailer Park. No fee is charged for camping at picnic areas at Second Mesa, west of the craft guild; Oraibi Wash, a mile east of New Oraibi at the bridge; and Pumpkin Hill, a mile west of New Oraibi.

GREAT Horned Owl Kachina wears buckskin robe, spies on Clown Kachinas.

COMPASSION Kachina soothes egos of children who have been punished.

CROW BRIDE wears wedding robe. Some believe she is mother of Kachinas.

LEFT-HANDED Kachina may represent left-handed hero from Hopi legend.

THE COLORFUL HOPI KACHINA DOLLS

Brightly colored Kachina dolls, presented to Hopi children by Kachina spirit impersonators who dance in the village plazas, are traditionally displayed from the rafters and walls of Hopi homes to help youngsters learn to identify the distinctive mask and costume of each Kachina spirit. Beyond the Hopi villages, the dolls are prized by collectors as some of the most meaningful and colorful examples of Indian art.

The pantheon of Kachina spirits includes about 250 individuals, ranging from a gift-bearing Santa Claus type to a ferocious black ogre who disciplines disobedient children. Many represent animals, plants or flowers, sky objects (sun, moon, and stars), or legendary figures from Hopi history. Other Kachinas are identified only by their particular ceremonial roles (runners, clowns, and escorts) or by some idiosyncrasy in costume or behavior. There is no fixed number of accepted Kachinas. New ones are introduced almost every year during Kachina ceremonies but return the next year only if they develop a popular following or bring about some beneficial effect.

The Kachina cult—belief in Kachina spirits, ceremonial function of masked Kachina impersonators, and carving of Kachina dolls—is shared by the Zuni Indians of New Mexico and by some of the pueblos along the Rio Grande; however, its most widespread acceptance is among the Hopis. Each Hopi individual is somehow involved in the cult, and the Hopi group is the only one that has developed the carving of Kachina

dolls into a popular and profitable art form.

Authentic Hopi-made Kachina dolls are carved from the roots of cottonwood trees. The cost depends almost entirely on the quality of workmanship. A well executed doll around 8 inches tall sells for about $30; elaborate detail work in the carving or costume design may push the price up as high as $50.

Several Hopi entrepreneurs manufacture a line of "tourist trade" Kachina dolls that are popular items in roadside curio shops. These simulated Kachina dolls (not true representations of a particular Kachina spirit) usually can be recognized by the simplicity of the lathe-turned body and by a tepee-shaped notch at the front of the solid base, representing the Kachina's feet. Genuine, hand-carved Kachinas have individually carved feet. Most simulated Hopi-made Kachina dolls are manufactured from cottonwood, but not necessarily from the root.

Even the simulated Kachina dolls have their imitators, made from balsa, pine, fir, and sometimes old broomsticks. Some imitations bear the label "Indian made" but are manufactured by non-Pueblo Indians who probably have never seen a real Hopi Kachina. Others come from as far away as Japan and may be made from ceramic materials, molded plastic, or plaster.

Your best assurance of authenticity is to buy directly from the Hopi crafts outlets on the reservation or from reputable Indian art dealers, traders, or museum shops.

THE WESTERN END OF NAVAJO COUNTRY

You complete your giant loop through the Navajo and Hopi reservations by rejoining U.S. 89 southwest of Tuba City. From here you can drive north to Lake Powell; or head south and, near Cameron, turn west on State 64 to the Little Colorado River gorge and then the Grand Canyon; or return on U.S. 89 to Flagstaff.

Lake Powell

Manmade Lake Powell, at the Navajo reservation's northern border, is being developed as a major recreation area for fishermen and water sports enthusiasts. The wilderness area stretching down from Lake Powell's south shore has been designated as Lake Powell Navajo Tribal Park, and the north shore comprises Glen Canyon National Recreation Area. The town of Page is the western entry to these areas; there are tourist accommodations here.

Lake Powell was formed by Glen Canyon Dam (renamed Dwight D. Eisenhower Dam in 1969), constructed from 1956 to 1964. You can take a self-guided tour of the dam and its power plant from the Carl Hayden Visitor Center on the canyon rim above the dam. From there it is 5 miles to Wahweap, the headquarters of Glen Canyon recreation area. Wahweap has a 178-unit campground, a trailer village, a motel, rental boats, and boat tours.

There are no paved roads within the tribal park on the lake's south shore, though the Navajos have plans to develop this area. The lake provides access to Rainbow Bridge National Monument, the largest known natural bridge in the world. Its inside span is 309 feet above the water. You also can reach the bridge from the land side (see page 22), but the waterway is the most popular approach; a short hike from the lake's edge takes you to the monument. Rainbow Bridge is near the base of Navajo Mountain, the highest spot on the reservation and a sacred place in Navajo mythology.

Little Colorado River Tribal Park

At the edge of the reservation next to Grand Canyon National Park is Little Colorado River Tribal Park. Take a dirt road which goes north from State Highway 64 for an expansive view of the Grand Canyon and of the narrower but still colorful and deep gorge of the Little Colorado. Twenty campsites are located in the park, but there has been no other development. A Navajo Arts and Crafts Guild outlet is located at the junction of State 64 and U.S. 89 below Cameron.

If you follow State 64 on west you will reach Grand Canyon Village on the south rim of Grand Canyon National Park.

GRAND CANYON INDIANS

The small cliff dwellings and pottery fragments they left in the walls of the Grand Canyon are evidence of Indians who lived here in prehistoric times. Long before Europeans discovered the canyon in 1540 these pueblo-dwelling groups had abandoned the area, but Indian life here has continued into modern times. The isolated Havasupai tribe lives on a tiny reservation deep in the Grand Canyon, while the Hualapai Indian Reservation borders the canyon to the south. Visits to these reservations will take you to spectacular views over and in the giant chasm.

Hualapai Indian Reservation

About a fourth of the Hualapai Indian Reservation consists of inaccessible mesas, gorges, and cliffs; the remainder is mostly rolling hills used as grazing land for cattle, the main source of income on the reservation. The center of Hualapai activities is the community of Peach Springs, on U.S. 66. A nine-member council meets here to govern the 700 Indians who live on the reservation. Groceries and craftwork can be purchased at a store in Peach Springs.

The Hualapai reservation has the only point of access to the Colorado River by car between Lee's Ferry (north of Navajo Bridge on U.S. 89A) and Lake Mead. This road, down Peach Springs Canyon north of Peach Springs, is sometimes closed by stormy weather; inquire locally about road conditions and directions.

A dirt road that leaves U.S. 66 about 2 miles west of Peach Springs leads to canyon overlooks at Honagi Point and Bachit Point (at the latter location is the abandoned upper station of an enormous aerial cableway built to remove bat guano from a cave near the bottom of the canyon, on the other side of the river). Take food, water, extra gas, and a good spare tire.

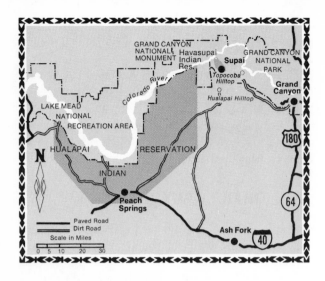

Havasupai Indian Reservation

If remote scenic areas hold a special appeal for you, then you will want to plan a trip to the narrow strip of land in rugged Havasu Canyon that serves as a home for 200 Havasupai Indians. The turquoise waters of Havasu Creek pass through the relatively flat floor of the canyon, irrigating Havasupai farm plots before dropping over three major waterfalls farther downstream. The creek gives the tribe its name—"people of the blue-green waters."

Access to the tiny reservation, which lies entirely within Grand Canyon National Park, is by two trails into the canyon. The most easily accessible is an 8-mile trail from Hualapai Hilltop, reached by a graded 60-mile road that leaves U.S. 66 about 7 miles east of Peach Springs. You can hike in (bring a canteen) or have an Indian guide meet you at the head of the trail with horses. The trail drops 2,000 feet to Supai Village, where there are overnight accommodations at two lodges (you do your own cooking) and a small grocery store. A national park service campground is situated 2½ miles down the canyon from the village; there is no charge for camping here, and water is available. Another campground is located about a mile below Supai near Navajo Falls. Firewood is scarce, so bring charcoal or buy it in Supai.

The second trail, 14 miles long, leads from Topocoba Hilltop. The 36-mile Rowe's Well road from Grand Canyon Village leads west to the trail's start, but at present this access is not recommended for vehicles other than four-wheel-drive or pickup trucks.

For information about lodgings and horseback trips, write to Havasupai Tourist Enterprise, Supai, Arizona 86435, or telephone in advance for reservations (602-448-2121, through Prescott). The horseback ride from Hualapai Hilltop costs about $18 to Supai or $20 to the campground, round trip.

Those who choose to hike into the canyon on foot are requested to obtain permission in advance by writing or by telephoning directly from Hualapai Hilltop (business hours only); a $2 trail use fee is charged, and each visitor must stop at the tourist manager's office in Supai to register.

Another means of getting to Havasu Canyon is by joining a pack trip; Joseph C. Wampler (Box 45, Berkeley, California 94701) conducts six-day package trips from Hualapai Hilltop.

There *is* one more way to reach the Havasupais —by helicopter. This is how five prefabricated houses were lowered into the reservation in June of 1969 as the first step of a federal program to provide adequate housing for the tribe. The new houses have indoor plumbing and are wired for electricity—though plans for bringing electricity to the canyon have not been completed.

Transporting tourists into the canyon is the major source of income for the Havasupais, who also farm and raise fruit. Their governing body includes four tribal council members and three hereditary chiefs. Late in August the tribe holds its annual Peach Festival, a harvest celebration.

SOUTH OF FLAGSTAFF

Two groups of Indian ruins south of Flagstaff—a cliff dwelling and a hilltop village—have been set aside as national monuments. If your trip takes you on to the city of Prescott, you can see the dances of the non-Indian Smoki People.

Montezuma Castle National Monument

A cliff dwelling dramatically situated against a limestone wall high above Beaver Creek in the Verde Valley is part of Montezuma Castle National Monument, just off Interstate 17 about 54 miles from Flagstaff. The monument is open from 7:30 A.M. to 7 P.M. daily from June through August, 8 A.M. to 6 P.M. from Labor Day through October, and 8 A.M. to 5 P.M. the rest of the year.

The five-story apartment-house dwelling known as Montezuma Castle had no connection with the Aztec ruler whose name it was given; early non-Indian settlers mistakenly thought the Aztecs had built it on their way to Mexico. You cannot enter Montezuma Castle, but you can see it from Sycamore Trail—the walk takes only a few minutes.

The prehistoric Verde Valley pueblo builders were Sinagua Indians who moved here from the north about 1100 A.D., joining Hohokam farmers already living here. The large hilltop and cliffside villages they built were begun about 1250 and seem to have been abandoned by 1450.

Seven miles northeast of Montezuma Castle is a large limestone sink from which the Indians diverted water into irrigation ditches. This is Montezuma Well, also part of the national monument. You still can see parts of the ancient irrigation canals and an excavated pit house.

About 4 miles south of Montezuma Castle is the community of Camp Verde, established in the 1860's as a military post during operations against the Apaches. Four of the adobe fort buildings still stand; one houses Fort Verde Museum.

Some 125 Indians live on a Yavapai reservation at Camp Verde.

Tuzigoot National Monument

During the thirteenth century Sinagua Indians like those who built Montezuma Castle lived in a pueblo on Tuzigoot Hilltop and in six other pueblos nearby. The hilltop is now a national monument, 20 miles northwest of Montezuma Castle on State Highway 279.

Tuzigoot's hilltop dwelling once contained about a hundred rooms and covered the summit and higher terraces of a long limestone ridge above the Verde Valley. Sometime in the 1400's the site was abandoned; Spanish soldiers who came in 1583 found it in ruins. Not until 1933 and 1934 was the site excavated.

The visitor center at Tuzigoot National Monument, open to the public between 8 A.M. and 5 P.M. daily, includes artifacts such as turquoise, mosaics, shell jewelry, and painted pottery.

Prescott

An annual ceremonial program and a museum of Indian artifacts in the city of Prescott, southwest

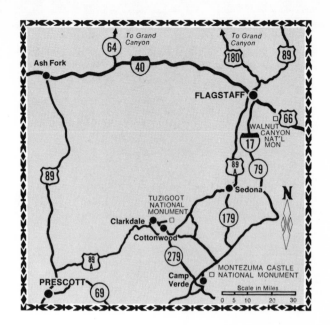

of Flagstaff on U.S. 89, are projects of a group of non-Indians called the Smoki People.

The Smoki perform their dances one Saturday early in August. Each year the program is different, but the climax is always the Smoki snake dance based on the famous rain dance of the Hopi Indians. The annual production grew out of a 1921 incident in which a group of Prescott men executed a not-very-serious snake dance as part of a fund-raising show. Hardly more than a burlesque, their performance nevertheless led some of them to undertake a study of the age-old songs and dances of various Indian tribes in order to recreate and perpetuate them.

The reaction among Indians has been mixed. Some object to the reenactment of ceremonies which are part of their religious rituals; others have assisted with the project.

The ceremonials take place at Yavapai County Fairgrounds. For information and tickets ($1.75 to $4 for adults, $1 to $4 for children; box seats also are available), write to The Smoki People, Box 123, or the Prescott Chamber of Commerce, Box 1147, Prescott, Arizona 86301.

The Smoki Museum is located on Arizona Avenue overlooking City Park in a pueblo-style structure. The museum is open from 10 A.M. to 4:30 P.M. weekdays, 1 to 5 P.M. Sundays from June 1 to September 1. Groups may see the museum by appointment during the rest of the year.

At the outskirts of Prescott is a small reservation on which about 70 Yavapai Indians live.

THE PUEBLOS

Living Villages...Abandoned Prehistoric Cities...Neighboring Ute Tribes

Prehistoric Southwest Indian culture reached its highest development among the ancient pueblo dwellers. You can visit their descendants in villages scattered across New Mexico in an arc from Zuni northeast into the Rio Grande Valley as far as Taos.

There are 18 Pueblo villages here, including both small clusters of a few gray adobe buildings and well-kept, multistoried dwellings. (A nineteenth group of Pueblo Indians, at Pojoaque, no longer has pueblo organization.) Named *Pueblos* by the Spaniards because they lived in compact, permanent villages, these Indians now have a total population of about 28,000 in New Mexico. In northern Arizona the Hopis are a pueblo-dwelling people (see page 30).

The Pueblo villages are near paved roads, and highway markers will show you where to turn off to reach them. The cities of Albuquerque and Santa Fe are in the heart of Pueblo country, and either can be a base for trips to the Indian villages. Nearby are the ruins of some of the most important prehistoric Pueblo cities, whose distinctive architecture remains an influence in the Southwest—you will see "pueblo-style" shopping centers, motels, even drive-in restaurants.

The Pueblo Indians are farmers by tradition, but today many of them work for wages in the nearby cities. Modern developments such as electricity—most of the pueblos now have it—and cement-block construction instead of adobe in some new structures are highly visible. Young people are likely to be dressed in the most current fashions, but in some of the villages women still wear cotton shawls and blanketlike woolen dresses draped over the right shoulder and under the left arm.

Modern times have brought a tinge of commercialism to some of the Pueblo villages, but you will still be fascinated by their impressive history, traditional way of life, colorful ceremonies, and skillfully made craftwork.

Each village is a self-contained political unit. Civil affairs generally are directed by a governor, assisting officers, and a council of leaders, while the priesthood controls religious and ceremonial matters. In prehistoric times the priests governed all the aspects of pueblo life, and even today they select the secular leaders in some of the pueblos. The pueblos are not organized together as a single tribal unit, but they do participate in an All-Pueblo Council which discusses matters concerning all of them.

There are three major language groups among the New Mexico Pueblos, and there are further divisions within these three. Keresan groups include the Western Keres pueblos of Acoma and Laguna and the Eastern Keres villages of Cochiti, Santa Domingo, San Felipe, Santa Ana, and Zia. The Tanoan language has three branches: Tiwa, spoken by Sandia, Isleta, Picuris, and Taos; Tewa, spoken by San Juan, Santa Clara, San Ildefonso, Nambe, and Tesuque; and Towa, spoken only by

ACOMA, founded perhaps a thousand years ago, is the oldest of New Mexico's Pueblo villages and may be oldest continually occupied town in United States.

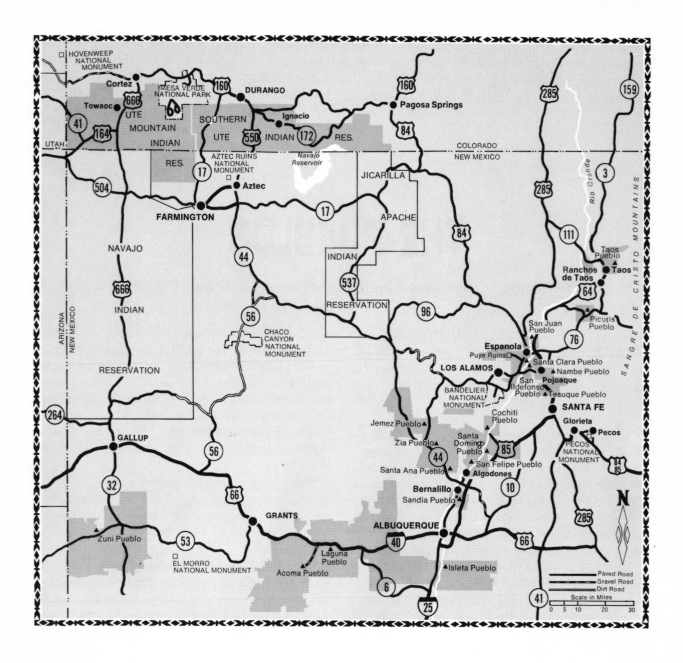

Jemez. Zuni pueblo comprises the Zunian linguistic family. Spanish is the adopted language most common to all the villages, although most of the younger villagers (especially the village leaders and craftsmen) also speak English.

The ancient city builders

The modern-day Pueblo Indians are descendants of prehistoric people known as the Anasazi. About 1,500 years ago this culture was in its early stages of development from nomadic groups to a semi-agricultural people whose fine baskets led archeologists to give them the name Basket-

makers. By about 700 A.D. pottery also was being made and village life was beginning; dwellings were sunken "pit houses." From about 700 to 1100, these houses evolved to more complex surface structures; the old pit houses, no longer used as dwellings, seem to have developed into sunken ceremonial chambers—the predecessors of kivas. Eventually multistoried houses were built.

The Anasazi culture reached its high point in most places sometime between the mid-eleventh century and the end of the thirteenth century. Its three main centers were at Chaco Canyon (architecture was most highly developed here), Mesa Verde (houses built in cliff openings led to the term Cliff Dwellers), and an area near Kayenta in northern Arizona; the ruins of each of these are a national park or monument.

Then, for some reason, the Pueblo people left the northern plateau country; by 1300 they had abandoned the great cities here. Though no one really knows why, it may have been a long drought that forced them to move, or attacks by warlike nomads may have driven them out.

By the time the first Spaniards arrived in the Southwest, pueblo culture was located roughly where it is found today—in the Rio Grande valley, the Zuni villages of western New Mexico, and the Hopi mesas of Arizona. Father Marcos de Niza led the first expedition into pueblo territory in 1539. The scout he sent ahead was killed at one of the Zuni pueblos and Father Marcos only glimpsed one of the villages, but he returned to Mexico with tales of riches which grew into the legend of the Seven Cities of Cibola. In 1540 Coronado and his army set out in search of these cities; he reached the Zuni villages but found nothing of the wealth he had been led to expect. Each village led the invaders on with promises of great riches *un poco mas alla*—"a little farther on." Forays to the Hopi villages, the Rio Grande valley, and on out to the region of the Plains Indians were no more productive. Finally in 1542 —after hundreds of Indians had been killed in skirmishes with the Spaniards — Coronado left the Southwest.

Other explorers followed him. One of the most important was Juan de Onate, who colonized New Mexico in 1598. Spanish missionaries established missions among the Indians during the seventeenth century.

An attempted revolt by the Indians in the mid-1600's was quickly crushed by the Spaniards, but in 1680 the independent pueblo villages joined forces and successfully threw off Spanish rule. The Pueblo Revolt forced the Spaniards to retreat to El Paso, and they did not return until 1692 when Diego de la Vargas reconquered the area—this time with little organized resistance. Many Indians moved from their villages in fear of Spanish retribution, some joining the Hopis (who were not reconquered) and some moving in among the Navajos.

Visiting a Pueblo village

When you enter a Pueblo village, go to see its governor to find out about any special regula- tions and ask any questions you have about the village and its activities. You may be met by a guide or a representative of the governor, or signs may be posted directing you to the governor's house; otherwise, anyone can tell you where he lives. The governor usually has been elected to his position because of his capabilities as an ambassador to the non-Indian world; usually he speaks English and is experienced in dealing with the public. If the governor is away (many of the men have jobs that take them away from the village during the day), his assistant or some member of his family will issue photography permits and collect fees. Some of the villages charge tourist fees and parking fees, and many charge photography fees.

Failure to comply with photography regulations could mean confiscation of your film (sometimes your camera) by village authorities. A few of the more conservative pueblos (such as Santa Domingo and San Felipe) prohibit all photography. Most prohibit photographs of the ceremonial kiva; religious processions and certain parts of the feast day celebrations may not be photographed in some villages. You also need to ask permission if you want to do any painting.

A Pueblo village, like any other community, is a collection of private homes. A photographer's permit is not a license to invade property. Do not enter any home without permission.

Most of the villages are open to tourists during the daylight hours; a few have hours posted for visitors. Weekdays are the best time to see village routine and visit craftmen's shops. Though some shops may be open daily during the summer, if you visit a village on an October weekend, you may find everyone has left to gather piñon nuts.

Festivals and ceremonies

Life in a Pueblo village today is a blend of two religious and cultural traditions. Dances that probably are not very different from those performed a thousand years ago in the ancient centers of Pueblo civilization now honor the village's patron saint. The costumes, the dances, and the ceremonial chants of the old Pueblo ancestors are intricately interwoven with a religious ritual that the Spanish padres brought to the Rio Grande Valley more than 400 years ago.

The colorful festivals, ceremonial processions, and ritual dances revolve around the village's two most important structures: the Christian church and the ceremonial kiva, important in Indian religion since ancient times. You are welcome to attend the church services usually held in conjunction with the various feast days, but ceremonial rituals held in the village kiva are decidedly out of bounds. That part of the ceremony the public is allowed to see usually takes place in the village plaza or along a central street.

Attention to detail is an extremely important part of each Pueblo ritual. The color, design, and arrangement of each costume must be exactly correct. Each procession and dance follows a carefully prescribed ritual routine.

Festivals usually are associated with the feast day of the patron saint of the village, but in actual practice the celebration is often shifted to the weekend closest the saint's day. Most festivals begin in mid-morning and continue until sunset. To verify dates of festivals and dances, check locally or write the New Mexico Commission on Indian Affairs, Room 111, La Posada Inn, 330 E. Palace Avenue, Santa Fe, New Mexico 87501. Some of the spontaneously scheduled observances also are open to the public and often are the most beautiful ceremonies.

Pueblo crafts

During the last 50 years there has been a revival of the old Pueblo arts and crafts. The success of such artists as Maria Martinez, the San Ildefonso potter whose polished black pottery with black matte design became popular about 1920, has inspired other Pueblo craftsmen to renew the skills of their ancestors.

Pottery is made in almost all of the villages, ranging from the museum-quality art works of San Ildefonso, Acoma, Santa Clara, and Zia pueblos to the what-not tourist trade items produced at Jemez and Isleta. A few of the older villagers in several pueblos now weave willow or yucca baskets in the tradition of their grandfathers, and some of the women at San Juan, Jemez, and Santa Clara pueblos are finding a ready acceptance for their fine embroidery and weaving. Zuni pueblo produces large quantities of excellent jewelry of silver with turquoise and shell. Silverwork is not one of the traditional crafts of the other pueblos, but several of the younger men have become accomplished silversmiths. Leatherwork, drums, and beadwork also are produced in some villages.

The average village craftsman often is quite shy about showing his work, but many of the established artists have their own retail shops and studios. The local Indian schools often are excellent sources of village craftwork; many of these schools—San Juan is a particularly good example — sponsor adult education classes that promote both the revival of the old arts and the development of new forms. Indians from the pueblos also attend the Institute of American Indian Arts in Santa Fe.

You will find endless arrays of so-called "Indian curios" displayed on blankets at most of the village festivals; many of these are strictly of trinket value, though some may be the work of Indian craftsmen from other pueblos who have their own shops in their home villages. Reputable Indian art shops in Taos, Santa Fe, and Albuquerque have excellent selections.

Camping, hunting, and fishing

Campgrounds are located at or near El Morro, Hovenweep, Aztec Ruins, Chaco Canyon, and Bandelier national monuments and Mesa Verde National Park (see section on each area for more information). You also may camp on a few of the Pueblo reservations.

Non-Indians may hunt and fish on certain reservation lands if they obtain tribal permits.

ALBUQUERQUE AND THE WESTERN PUEBLOS

In the Southwest, it often is only a short distance between bustling urban centers and centuries-old village cultures. The city of Albuquerque is a good starting point for visits to the three Western Pueblos—Laguna, Acoma, and Zuni. In this group are the newest, the oldest, and the most populous of New Mexico's pueblos.

Albuquerque itself offers several chances to see aspects of Indian culture. Pueblo and Navajo Indians run an Indian village at the annual state fair held here in late September, featuring display booths and daily programs of Indian dances. Another opportunity to see Indian dances and crafts is at the New Mexico Arts and Crafts Fair held the first weekend in August in Albuquerque.

A historic orientation to the Southwest Indian cultures is presented at the University of New

THE ART OF PUEBLO POTTERY

Native Southwest pottery is built up of coils rather than being formed on a potter's wheel. The straight-sided coiled pot is then shaped from within (the traditional tool is a curved piece of gourd shell) and scraped smooth. Next comes the application of several coats of fine clay mixed with water—called the slip. Then the pot is polished until it is shiny, and a design is painted on with a yucca-leaf brush before the vessel is oven-fired at a low temperature. (This pottery is not glazed and does not hold water.)

Each pueblo has developed certain shapes, ways of applying the slip, design patterns, and firing methods. Even the type of clay available to the village makes a difference in the appearance of the pottery it produces. The following are leading pottery-making pueblos and styles:

- Acoma pottery is distinguished by its thin walls and light weight. It is polychrome, usually with a white slip, reddish base, and red and black designs—either geometric forms or flowers and birds.

- Zuni (where most of the villagers have become silversmiths instead of potters) has specialized in pottery owl figurines, decorated with black and red on a white slip.

- Zia's graceful designs—birds, deer, and stylized floral patterns—have long made the village a trend setter among the pueblo potters. Red and black designs are painted on a white or tan slip.

- Cochiti has recently introduced imaginatively formed human figurines which have become very popular. Other Cochiti pottery—bird and animal figures as well as bowls—has black designs on a pinkish cream slip.

- San Ildefonso and Santa Clara both produce polished red and black ware with matte designs, sometimes deeply carved. The black sheen is produced when smoke is allowed to smother the pot during the firing process. Santa Clara pottery tends to be a bit more massive than that of San Ildefonso. San Ildefonso also makes some pottery with white, black, and pink designs on red slips, and Santa Clara has developed a design style using white and light red on dull red slips.

- San Juan's most distinctive pottery is light brown with an incised design. Polychrome pottery and polished red ware are made, too.

- Picuris and Taos both make unpainted vessels for use in cooking. Mica content in the clay gives the light brown pots a metallic appearance.

- Hopi potters make polychrome ware—black, red-orange, and white designs on a cream or orange slip. An undecorated utility ware is used for cooking by many Hopi women.

Mexico's Museum of Anthropology, open Monday through Saturday from 10 A.M. to 4 P.M. during summer, 9 A.M. to 4 P.M. in winter; the museum is on University N.E. about three blocks north of Central. Other exhibits dealing with Indian history can be seen at the Museum of Albuquerque (south end of Yale Boulevard) from 10 A.M. to 5 P.M. Tuesday through Saturday, 1 to 5 P.M. Sunday; admission is 25 cents for adults, 10 cents for children, free on Sunday. Two more Indian museums are located at the Santa Fe Railway Depot and Wright's Trading Post, 616 Central Avenue S.W.

From Albuquerque, drive west on U.S. Highway 66-Interstate 40, a streamlined route that offers sweeping vistas as you top long rises on your way to Laguna and Acoma. Then State Highway 53 (all-paved) is a pleasant drive through wooded country to Zuni pueblo.

Laguna Pueblo

The most recently organized pueblo and one of the most populous is Laguna, located just off U.S. 66-Interstate 40 about 45 miles west of Albuquerque. Laguna was founded in 1699 and is the mother pueblo for a group of nearby communities. Of the total population of about 5,000, some 1,300 live at Laguna itself.

The oldest section of Laguna, built on a sandstone bluff overlooking the Rio San Jose, is right around the plaza and just south of it. The mission church was built about 1700.

Laguna is known as one of the most progressive pueblos. Uranium and marble deposits on the reservation are a source of tribal income. Crafts made here include some embroidery and limited quantities of basketry and pottery resembling that of Acoma.

Public fishing is permitted at Paguate Reservoir; you can purchase a reservation fishing permit at the Laguna Police office.

Acoma Pueblo

Spectacularly located atop an isolated 400-foot sandstone mesa 50 miles west of Albuquerque is Acoma, the pueblo known as Sky City. Acoma, occupied for at least a thousand years, claims to supersede the Hopi pueblo of Oraibi as the oldest continuously occupied town in this country. To reach the ancient community, leave U.S. 66-Interstate 40 at Paraje for a 14-mile drive south on State Highway 23. You will see the Enchanted Mesa—a long, narrow butte supposed to have been the

ANCIENT ACOMA pueblo's location on top of a 400-foot-high mesa gives it the name "Sky City."

abode of the Acoma Indians until an earthquake rendered the summit inaccessible.

Today most of the 2,700 Acoma Indians live in the farming villages of Acomita and McCarty's but return to the mesa-top pueblo for ceremonial occasions, such as a fiesta on September 2, a corn dance in June, and other dances at Christmas and Easter. Acoma is well known for its thin-walled, well designed pottery.

You can either drive to the top of the mesa (there is a parking fee) or climb up on a foot trail. A visitor's fee of $1 per adult or 50 cents per child age 6 through 16 is charged for admission to Acoma; you may visit between 6 A.M. and 6 P.M. Once at the top you will see ancient structures and newer dwellings built to the pattern of the old (but with screen doors and glass instead of native mica for windows). The imposing mission church, started in 1628, has walls 10 feet thick and 60 feet high. Everything used in its construction—including a timber 40 feet long and 14 inches square, from the distant Cebolleta Mountains—had to be carried to the top of the rock by the Indians, as did the thousands of basketfuls of earth for the burial ground.

Public fishing is permitted on the Acoma reservation at Mesa Hill Lake and San Jose River. Fishing permits can be purchased at the lake; there are picnic facilities and a general store here.

El Morro National Monument

The towering sandstone bluff that served both as a landmark and a journal for early Southwest travelers is a worthwhile stop along State Highway 53 en route to Zuni pueblo. Drive south from Interstate 40 at the turnoff to El Morro National Monument just past Grants. The country becomes greener and the air crisper as you come into juniper and pine stands.

The craggy, pink-brown mass of El Morro—Spanish for "bluff" or "headland"—is 53 miles from Grants. Early Indian hunters, Spanish conquistadors, and wagon-train pioneers found shelter beneath its steep cliffs, and over the centuries travelers carved their names into the soft sandstone rock. The oldest inscription reads "The Governor Don Juan de Onate passed this way from his discovery of the Sea of the South on April 16, 1605." But Onate was not the first to find refuge at El Morro. Ancient Indian petroglyphs on the cliff wall and ruins of pueblo dwellings on top of the 200-foot-high rock predate him. By the time the Spaniards arrived, the Indian dwellings had already been abandoned.

A guide-yourself trail leads along the base of the cliff, with its many inscriptions, and to the pueblo ruins (mostly unexcavated) on top. The monument is open from 8 A.M. to 5 P.M. At the visitor center you can view exhibits describing the area's history. Admission is $1 per carload.

A small campground is located here.

Zuni Pueblo

The legendary Seven Cities of Cibola lured Coronado to the Southwest in 1540 in search of treasure. All but one of those sites were abandoned long ago; the exception is the village of Zuni, which stands where the pueblo of Halana once stood.

Today this quiet community is the largest of New Mexico's Pueblo villages and the center of population for the 5,500 Indians who live on the Zuni Indian Reservation. In addition to the main village there are smaller farming communities called Ojo Caliente, Tehopo, Pescado, and Nutria.

Zuni pueblo is located on State Highway 53 near the New Mexico-Arizona border. To get tourist information and purchase a photography permit, go to the Tribal Council-Tribal Police building (turn off the main road opposite the post office, where a sign directs you to the Zuni Craftsmen Cooperative Association). You can arrange for a guide for a small fee; this is particularly helpful if you are interested in visiting some of the silversmiths at work in their homes. Silver jewelry also can be seen in various stages of production at the Craftsmen Cooperative Association workshop behind the tribal office building; the sales shop is open from 8 A.M. to 5 P.M. every day from March to September, weekdays only during the rest of the year.

Some 1,000 Zuni residents are silversmiths, most of them on a part-time basis. Both men and women make the famous Zuni jewelry; much of the Indian jewelry sold throughout the United States is created here. A limited number of pottery vessels and ceramic owls are made, and some stone fetishes and Kachina dolls are carved.

In addition to having a reputation as fine craftsmen, Zuni Indians are famous as fire fighters. They were the first group trained as fire-fighting experts in a nationwide program.

Few multistoried buildings remain. New homes

BEEHIVE-SHAPED ovens like these at Zuni pueblo are still used for baking in the Indian villages.

are being built on individual lots from stone or cement blocks with pitched rather than flat roofs. You will see some of the oldest structures near the recently restored adobe mission church.

Native religious ceremonies are an important part of Zuni life. Masked public dances are presented by the six kiva organizations, most frequently during a three-month period at the winter and summer solstice. The public also may attend the spectacular house-blessing ceremony and Shalako dance performed by 10-foot-tall masked figures sometime in late November or early December.

You may want to visit Hawikuh Ruins, the remains of one of the pueblos seen by the first Spanish explorers, on a high point of land about 15 miles southwest of Zuni pueblo. Get detailed directions to the ruins before you leave town.

You may fish and hunt (deer and birds) on the reservation if you obtain a tribal permit, sold at the tribal offices and at a number of stores in Gallup, Grants, and Albuquerque. There is a campground east of Zuni village, and camping permits are $1 per night or $3 per week.

THE RIO GRANDE VALLEY PUEBLOS

Fifteen of the Pueblo villages lie in the Rio Grande Valley, from Isleta in the arid country south of Albuquerque to Taos in New Mexico's northern mountains. You can visit several in a single short trip or make a more leisurely tour of the entire valley.

Isleta Pueblo

Isleta is large both in area and in population. The southernmost of the existing Rio Grande valley pueblos, it is located 13 miles south of Albuquerque. Its population is about 2,400, including two colonies downriver from the main village and a settlement called Oraibi, founded by a conservative group that left Laguna pueblo about 1880.

Isleta pueblo has many streets, a circular kiva, and a mission church originally built before 1629. It is not known just when Isleta was founded; Spaniards reported a village they called Isleta in 1540, and the pueblo may still be located at the original site or it may have been moved.

Agriculture, land leases, and wage work in Albuquerque provide income for residents of Isleta. Some pottery and jewelry are made at the pueblo, but the "Isleta" pottery—red, with black and red designs on white—is actually made by women of Oraibi, the Laguna colony at Isleta.

Ceremonies at the pueblo include *chongo* races (ritualistic relays) in late March and early April, a fiesta on September 4, and ceremonies at Christmas.

Sandia Pueblo

Low one-story adobes make up the small pueblo of Sandia, located 14 miles north of Albuquerque off U.S. Highway 85. The pueblo has been occupied since about 1300 and was visited by Coronado in 1540. During the 1680 Pueblo Rebellion, people from Sandia moved to the Hopi villages, though evidence that the pueblo has been continuously occupied suggests that some Indians remained or soon returned. In 1742 the Sandia Indians returned from the Hopi region.

The oldest part of the pueblo—much of it in ruin—can be seen between the church and the highway. Sandia has a population of about 250. Residents are farmers and wage workers in nearby towns. No crafts are being produced.

The pueblo's annual festival on June 13 includes a corn dance. Other ceremonies are held throughout the year. You may visit Sandia from 10 A.M. to 4 P.M.

Santa Ana Pueblo

Santa Ana pueblo usually is left in the charge of caretakers, since most of the 450 Santa Ana Indians live in settlements along the Rio Grande. Poor land and lack of water necessitated their move from the mother pueblo, located on the north side of Jemez Creek.

You reach Santa Ana from State Highway 44 about 8 miles northwest of Bernalillo; access to the pueblo is by a dirt road fording Jemez Creek. The pueblo often is closed to visitors. The Indians return for ceremonial occasions, such as a feast day July 26.

The present pueblo dates from about 1700. An earlier village was destroyed during the Spanish occupation of the late seventeenth century.

Little craftwork is done by the Santa Ana Indians, though a very small amount of pottery is produced. Some woven belts, carved wooden animal figures, and wood crosses are made.

Zia Pueblo

Built high on a mesa overlooking Jemez Creek, Zia pueblo is reached via State Highway 44 about 16 miles northwest of Bernalillo and about 8 miles beyond Santa Ana pueblo. The pueblo has been occupied since about 1300, when Indians moved here from farther up Jemez Creek. The location is a barren one, offering little good farmland; some sheep and goats are raised. Many of the 500 Zia Indians work off the reservation.

The pueblo was built around a plaza. One of the circular kivas was destroyed by fire in 1948 during one of the recurring periods of factionalism in the village. The mission church at Zia is a massive, balconied structure.

Zia is known for its fine pottery. An ancient sun symbol used in Zia pottery was incorporated into the design of the New Mexico state flag.

The pueblo's annual fiesta is August 15.

Jemez Pueblo

Just off State Highway 4 about 25 miles northwest of Bernalillo is Jemez Pueblo, the only remaining Towa-speaking group. Once there were many Towa villages north of the present site of Jemez, probably founded sometime during the last half of the sixteenth century.

A well kept pueblo, Jemez today consists mostly of one-story buildings; a hundred years ago there were many two-story structures.

Jemez dancers are well known for their skill. The annual fiesta is held on November 12. Buffalo and hoop dances are performed during the winter and corn dances in August. On August 2 descendants of Indians who moved to Jemez from Pecos (now Pecos National Monument—see page 54) about 1838 observe their feast day, and the Pecos bull dance is performed.

There are about 1700 Jemez Indians. Agriculture is the chief occupation. Some fine plaited yucca baskets are produced by Jemez women. Most of the pottery made here is styled for the tourist trade — brightly decorated with poster paints. Other Jemez crafts include embroidery, water color painting, and drum-making.

Two recreation areas are operated by the Jemez pueblo. One is Holy Ghost Spring, 40 miles north of Bernalillo just east of State 44; the other is Sheep Lake, near the pueblo. Fishing permits may be purchased at the pueblo or at several nearby locations. Permits for big game hunting must be obtained from the pueblo governor.

San Felipe Pueblo

One of the most conservative pueblos, San Felipe is especially noted for its impressive ceremonial observances. Its famous corn dance is held May 1, with hundreds of dancers participating. On

---

ZUNI, NAVAJO, AND HOPI SILVERSMITHS

The Zunis, the Navajos, and the Hopis each have developed their own distinctive styles of silver jewelry.

The technique most characteristic of Zuni jewelry is *inlay* or *mosaic*, in which pieces of blue turquoise, black jet, red coral, and white mother of pearl are carefully fitted together and glued onto a solid base. This style led to the development of *channel* work; a raised silver grid design separates individual stones, and the entire surface is smoothed. The oldest form used by the Zunis probably is the setting of single stones into individual bases, which led to *cluster* settings of small stones and then the finely cut stones of *needlepoint*. The most recent Zuni development is *nugget* jewelry; stones are polished in their natural shapes and set in a contoured silver base.

Navajo silversmiths make both *hammered* and *sandcast* jewelry. In the first method, silver is hammered into a thin layer to be cut and then filed or stamped with a design. For sandcasting, a design is carved into a piece of soft rock; melted silver is poured into this mold. The hardened piece of silver, distinguished by a ridge formed by the wedge-shaped groove of the mold, is then filed and polished.

The most popular Hopi silverwork technique is *overlay*. A design is cut out of a sheet of silver, and then the sheet is soldered onto a second sheet of silver. The cut-out area is blackened.

JEWELRY at left is Zuni channel work (top), needlepoint (left), and inlay. Navajo work, center, is hammered and sandcast (bottom); earring is squash blossom design. At right are Hopi overlay pieces.

Christmas Eve, deer and buffalo impersonators dance.

San Felipe pueblo is located about 30 miles north of Albuquerque. Signs mark the turnoff west from U.S. 85-Interstate 25 about 10 miles north of Bernalillo.

The present pueblo was built on the west bank of the Rio Grande early in the eighteenth century (more recently some dwellings have been built east of the river as well). Earlier villages of the same native and then Spanish name were located elsewhere.

One interesting feature of San Felipe pueblo is the sunken plaza—the main part is three feet below the level at the edge. The pueblo also has an unusually fine mission church.

About 1,500 Indians are included in San Felipe's population. Craftwork is limited.

Santa Domingo Pueblo

Tradition rules the lives of the Indians of Santa Domingo, known as the most conservative pueblo. The pattern of life here is little different from what it was when the Spaniards arrived.

You can reach Santa Domingo by a paved road branching to the pueblo from State 22 or by a secondary road south of Cochiti pueblo. Santa Domingo is located on the east bank of the Rio Grande and is one of the largest pueblos. There are two circular kivas and a mission church unusual because of its mural paintings. Most of the present pueblo has been built since 1886, when a flood destroyed much of an old settlement built about 1700. There may have been an earlier village as well.

Some 2,200 people are included in Santa Domingo's population. Farming is the primary occupation of the men. Many of the women produce pottery, ranging in quality from very good to inferior. Today much of the pottery is copied from that made in other pueblos. Shell and turquoise jewelry, including bead necklaces, is a specialty of Santa Domingo craftsmen; silver jewelry is also produced.

The native religious structure is very important in Santa Domingo and has a strong influence over the government of the pueblo. Ceremonials include the dramatic corn dance August 4 and dances at New Year's and Easter; a small fee is charged visitors who wish to attend.

Cochiti Pueblo

A reputation for producing the finest drums in the Southwest has been earned by Cochiti pueblo, and many other Indians obtain their ceremonial drums from Cochiti drummakers. Rawhide is stretched over the ends of hollowed-out cottonwood log sections, and the drums may then be painted or left undecorated.

Cochiti is a pueblo of one and two-story communal apartment houses built around a plaza. There are two circular kivas. The pueblo is located on the west side of the Rio Grande, and you reach it by turning from U.S. 85 onto State 22 about 40 miles north of Albuquerque.

The pueblo has been occupied since 1250 or perhaps earlier. Some of the 700 Cochiti Indians are farmers, and many work off their reservation. Crafts produced in Cochiti include pottery, leather moccasins and bags, and beadwork as well as drums.

A fiesta and corn dance is held on July 14.

You may fish in the Rio Grande and hunt for doves and ducks on the Cochiti reservation if you obtain permission from the governor.

Tesuque Pueblo

Ten miles north of Santa Fe, just off U.S. 285-64, is the small pueblo of Tesuque. Native ceremonials retain their importance to residents of this pueblo. Tesuque's harvest dance on November 12 is among ceremonies at the pueblo.

Some of the buildings around the central plaza are two stories high. The simple mission church dates from 1915. The pueblo was founded about 1250.

Watercolor-decorated pottery bowls and figurines are made in Tesuque. The making of traditional-style pottery has largely been abandoned in favor of gaudy curios.

Tesuque is the smallest of the Tewa-speaking groups, with a population of about 230. Farming is the principal occupation. The pueblo is open to visitors from 8 A.M. to 5 P.M.

Pojoaque

No longer recognizable as a pueblo organization, Pojoaque nevertheless is an Indian reservation, located between the pueblos of Nambe and

CHURCH at Santa Domingo, built after flood in 1886 destroyed older structure, is distinguished by murals painted on front. Each pueblo has a mission church.

Tesuque. There are about 70 people living in the village of Pojoaque.

Nambe Pueblo

A small, back-road pueblo that has become almost indistinguishable from a Spanish-American village, Nambe is notable for its annual fiesta October 4 and for nearby Nambe Falls. To reach the pueblo, turn west onto State Highway 4 at Pojoaque, 16 miles north of Santa Fe on U.S. Highway 84-285. About 5 miles farther a road marker shows where to turn onto the short dirt access road to Nambe pueblo.

Nambe's circular gray adobe kiva establishes the village's identity as an Indian settlement. Nambe has been occupied since 1300 or even earlier, but today it has lost much of its Indian character. Farming and wage work off the reservation provide income for Nambe's 200 members. Few arts and crafts are produced now, although a nearby manufacturing plant employs many of the pueblo residents to produce aluminum tableware named after the pueblo.

Colorful dances are performed in Nambe's plaza on the October 4 feast day. Another festival has been held in recent years on July 4 at Nambe Falls, a recreational area on Nambe Creek above the pueblo. Fishing and picnicking are permitted at the falls; a small entrance fee is charged.

San Ildefonso Pueblo

Though the San Ildefonso Indians number only about 300, their pueblo has been made famous by the excellent pottery which has been produced here. San Ildefonso is the home of Maria Martinez, probably the most famous Indian potter, who developed the black-on-black style for which the village became known. Today there are a number of fine potters and painters here.

San Ildefonso is a well kept pueblo which can be reached from State 4. The pueblo is built around two plazas divided by a block of buildings (factionalism resulted in half of the residents moving to the newer South Plaza area in about 1910 while the rest remained in the North Plaza). Each has a rectangular kiva, and a circular kiva is located in the South Plaza.

The pueblo has been occupied since about 1300, though there has been some change in the exact location of the village. The present mission church, facing the governor's office, was built about 1905 on the site of an earlier church.

KIVA at San Ildefonso is in pueblo's South Plaza; another plaza is behind row of buildings in background.

MATRIARCH of San Juan pueblo makes pottery that has won her many awards at Indian fairs.

Many San Ildefonso Indians have jobs at the Los Alamos atomic energy center—an interesting contrast to their ancient village and traditional way of life.

San Ildefonso's annual fiesta is held January 23 and includes buffalo and Comanche dances. A corn dance September 8 is among other ceremonies here. The pueblo may be visited from 9 A.M. to 5 P.M.

Santa Clara Pueblo

A visit to Santa Clara pueblo can be combined with a trip to cliff dwellings which the Santa Clara Indians claim as their ancestral home. The pueblo is 2 miles south of Espanola off State 30, and the Puye Ruins are 3¹/₂ miles south and 9 miles west of the pueblo, on State Highway 5.

Residents of Santa Clara act as custodians of the Puye Ruins, dramatically situated on the eastern edge of the Pajarito Plateau overlooking the Rio Grande Valley. A small admission charge is collected at the ruins, and you may explore them at your leisure. Cavelike rooms honeycombing the soft volcanic cliffs and single-story and multistoried mesa-top structures were probably occupied from the late 1200's until the middle 1500's. Part of the old pueblo has been restored, but most of it consists of roofless masonry walls that only hint at the extent of the original village. A visitor center is maintained at the ruins during the summer, and during one weekend in late July a public festival is held.

Santa Clara pueblo itself most likely dates from sometime in the fourteenth century. The 750 Santa Clara Indians, many of whom are employed at the Los Alamos atomic energy center, are known for their excellent pottery.

On August 12 Santa Clara pueblo celebrates its fiesta. Buffalo dances are performed on June 8.

Near Puye Ruins is the Santa Clara Canyon recreational area (11 miles west of Espanola off State 30), where you can picnic, camp, or fish—there are four small lakes plus Santa Clara Creek. You can obtain daily picnicking, fishing, and camping permits at the ranger station in the canyon or purchase a seasonal permit which covers all three. Horses can be rented.

San Juan Pueblo

The first Spanish settlement in New Mexico was established across the Rio Grande from San Juan pueblo in 1598. Initially hospitable to the Spaniards, San Juan pueblo later produced the leader of the 1680 Pueblo Revolt.

PICURIS kiva is in old section of village where ruins have been excavated.

NAMBE festival is observed with colorful dances. Pueblo culture is mixture of ancient Indian beliefs, rites introduced by Spanish priests.

The pueblo is about 5 miles north of the town of Espanola on the east bank of the Rio Grande. Its population of 1,275 includes many who have left to find jobs outside the reservation.

Women of San Juan make good-quality pottery. Wood carvings, embroidery, beadwork, and leatherwork also are produced.

The pueblo is noted for performances of *Los Matachines,* a Mexican-Indian dance. The annual fiesta is held June 24.

You can fish in the Rio Grande for the 5 miles it crosses the San Juan reservation, and you can hunt for birds. You must obtain reservation permits for fishing and hunting.

Picurís Pueblo (San Lorenzo)

The small village of Picurís is located in the mountain country about 20 miles south of Taos on the north bank of the Rio Pueblo. You can reach the pueblo from the south via State Highway 75 or State Highway 76 or from Taos via State Highway 3.

Picurís was settled about 1250 by Indians from a pueblo now known as Pot Creek ruin (near Talpa on State 3). The excavated remains of the original buildings at Picurís are open to visitors,

and guides are available to show them to you. The northern section of the pueblo contains the oldest structures. One recently-built feature of "new" Picurís is a community center decorated with murals. Picurís is open to visitors from 8 A.M. to 5 P.M.; a tourist fee is charged.

Potters in Picurís make unusual cooking vessels from mica-infused clay which produces a metallic appearance. Cooks value the earthen vessels as bean pots.

About 170 Indians are included in the population of Picurís. They raise crops and graze livestock on their small reservation. A small reservoir and the Rio Pueblo provide fishing; visitors may obtain permits to fish here.

The pueblo's annual fiesta is August 10.

Taos Pueblo

The most famous of all the pueblos and perhaps the most beautifully situated is Taos, where some of the communal dwellings are as high as five stories. The northernmost pueblo, Taos is about 65 miles north of Santa Fe.

There are three Taos communities. The Indian pueblo is three miles beyond the town of Taos, with its artists' colony and resorts. A few miles

APARTMENT dwelling at Taos rises picturesquely to five stories. This is North House, separated by creek from South House section of pueblo.

south on U.S. 64 is Ranchos de Taos village and a much painted, much photographed church.

The pueblo, picturesquely situated against New Mexico's highest mountains, is divided into two parts by Taos Creek (several footbridges cross the creek). A portion of North House is five stories high, while South House reaches four stories in height. Taos is the only pueblo with a surrounding wall. There are seven circular kivas. The present pueblo village was built about 1700; an older village, destroyed by fire, was located northeast of the present site on both sides of the creek and was visited by Alvarado in 1540.

The multistoried Taos dwellings are an impressive backdrop for the traditional ceremonies performed at the pueblo. The annual fiesta on September 30 is preceded the evening before by a sunrise dance. Ceremonies at Christmas, January 1, January 6, and other times include corn dances, eagle dances, turtle dances, horsetail dances, ceremonial races, and non-religious social dances.

Because of its northern location, Taos adapted certain traits of dress and ceremonies characteristic of Plains Indians with whom they traded.

The Taos reservation provides farm land and grazing areas for livestock, including bison.

Crafts at Taos include some leatherwork (especially deerskin moccasins) and mica-infused pottery similar to that made in Picurís.

At the entrance to the pueblo an official will collect a parking fee; you also can purchase a photography permit from him. The pueblo is open to visitors from 8 A.M. to 6 P.M.

SANTA FE

Situated right in the heart of Pueblo country is historic Santa Fe, New Mexico's capital. Here you can browse through museums to learn about both ancient and modern Indian cultures, see the work of young artists at an Indian school, and visit some of the best Indian craft shops in the Southwest.

Each year Indians from all over the state display their handiwork at the Indian Arts and Crafts Market held in Santa Fe on the third Saturday and Sunday in August. Craftwork is displayed on blankets under the portal of the Palace of the Governors and under brightly colored awnings that line the Santa Fe Plaza across the street. Prize ribbons hang from work judged outstanding by a group of specialists in Indian art. In the patio of the Palace authentic Indian dances are presented each day; admission is charged. The Southwestern Association on Indian Affairs sponsors the market and dance programs.

Museum of New Mexico

Indian life in the Southwest is traced back for thousands of years at the Museum of New Mexico in the Palace of the Governors, located directly across Plaza Avenue from the Santa Fe Plaza. The Palace itself has a fascinating history; constructed in 1610, it is the oldest public building in the country and once was the principal center of government in the Southwest. Following the Pueblo Revolt of 1680, Indians lived in the Palace for 13 years and made it into a multistoried pueblo. Today Indian craftsmen come to the Palace each day to spread out jewelry and pottery on blankets under the portal to sell.

The Palace now houses part of one of the Southwest's finest museums. The east end contains exhibits relating to history of the building and the state; the west end takes you back 20,000 years and explains Southwest history through the development of the major Indian cultures, illustrated by an extensive collection of artifacts. Behind the patio of the Palace is the Hall of the Modern Indian, where you learn about the costumes, food, dwellings, and arts and crafts of contemporary Southwest Indians.

The museum's research laboratory periodically has special exhibits of both contemporary Indian materials and archeological collections. Across the street from the Palace you can see Indian paintings at the Fine Arts Building; the International Folk Art Building, located 2 miles south of the plaza off Pecos Road, has a collection of Indian craftwork. Each May there are special painting and crafts shows at these two buildings, and Indian artists are among those exhibiting.

The Museum of New Mexico is open from 9 A.M. to 5 P.M. Monday through Saturday and 2 to 5 P.M. Sunday from May 14 to Sept. 12, closed Mondays the rest of the year. Admission is free.

Museum of Navaho Ceremonial Art

An octagonal building symbolizing a Navajo hogan houses the Museum of Navaho Ceremonial Art, located at 704 Camino Lejo in Santa Fe. On display at the privately-endowed museum are replicas of sandpaintings, ritual objects, pottery, basketry, carvings, and jewelry. In addition, a research library contains books and manuscripts related to the Navajos and even a file of Navajo chants.

You can visit the museum from 9 A.M. to 5 P.M. Tuesday through Saturday, 2 to 5 P.M. Sunday. Admission is free.

Institute of American Indian Arts

Students at a unique school in Santa Fe express their Indian cultural traditions through their work in the arts. The Institute of American Indian Arts, established by the Bureau of Indian Affairs in 1962, offers studies in creative writing, drama, music, dance, textiles, painting, ceramics, metalwork and lapidary, sculpture, photography, and commercial arts.

The Institute is an accredited high school with an extensive program of art electives and two years of postgraduate work. Some 250 Indian students (ages 14 through 22) from all across the country study here. Since the Institute opened, more than 80 tribes have been represented in its student body.

The school is located on Cerillos Road on the old Santa Fe Indian School campus. You can visit its adobe buildings and see the school in operation from the day after Labor Day to the end of May, 8:30 A.M. to 4 P.M. Monday through Friday. Guided tours are conducted upon request, and sometimes you can see students at work. A gift shop, named Hookstone, is run by students as part of a class in sales methods; student-made paintings, pottery, and jewelry can be seen and purchased here.

Indian customs are stressed in student activities throughout the year. One popular event is the Indian Foods Day. For this occasion, the traditional dwelling structures of various tribes are constructed, and students go from hogan to tepee to wickiup to sample typical foods of each group.

THE ANCIENT CITY RUINS

The ruins of the cities that dominated early Southwest culture but were abandoned long before the first Spaniards arrived are an impressive record of the achievements of the prehistoric Anasazi people. Seeing some of these deserted cities is an important counterpart to your visits to the modern-day pueblo villages.

Mesa Verde National Park

You can trace the development of Indian life at Mesa Verde from the ruins of early pit houses to terraced mesa-top pueblo villages and the spectacular cliff dwellings. About 2000 mesa-top ruins and 200 cliff dwellings have been surveyed throughout Mesa Verde National Park, perhaps the best known of the prehistoric pueblo sites.

Entrance to the park is 10 miles east of Cortez, on U.S. Highway 160. Start your visit at the Navajo Hill Visitor Center (open summers only) or the Chapin Mesa Museum (open all year).

Indians lived in the Mesa Verde region for thirteen centuries. Development of pueblo dwellings here took place from about 750 to 1100 A.D., and during the next two centuries the culture reached its peak. The flourishing mesa pueblos began to be abandoned after 1200 in favor of more sheltered (but less comfortable) locations in the enormous niches of Mesa Verde's ramparts, perhaps for protection from enemy attacks. By 1300 the entire area was abandoned.

You may visit the mesa-top ruins on your own, but you may enter cliff dwellings only under the supervision of a ranger. Rangers conduct trips to various groups of ruins during summer, to Spruce Tree House only in winter (weather permitting). Bus trips leave from Far View Terrace and Spruce Tree Terrace; cost is $3 per person.

Two short loop drives on the Ruins Road cross a relic-rich area of Chapin Mesa, which contains some of the most spectacular sections of ruins. On one of the loops you see Square Tower House, a series of excavations showing the sequence of pueblo architectural development, and the dramatically situated Sun Temple. The other takes you to Balcony House and Cliff Palace, the park's most famous ruin. Cliff Palace has eight floor levels and housed 200 people.

Hikers can follow the three-mile trail to Pictograph Point; obtain a hiking permit at the Chief Ranger's office.

Cabins and motel accommodations are operated within the park by the Mesa Verde Company (Box 277, Mancos, Colorado 81329), from mid-May to mid-October. The Morfield Campground has over 450 tent and trailer sites and is open from about May 1 to October 15.

Entrance fee for Mesa Verde National Park is $1 per day per car.

Hovenweep National Monument

Six clusters of ruins scattered across the Four Corners country are maintained as Hovenweep National Monument.

The Hovenweep ruins are noted for their tall towers, built about 1200 to defend the small villages against nomadic invaders. The villages were abandoned by about 1300.

The Square Tower Canyon group is the most accessible of the ruins; you reach it via a 27-mile graded road from Pleasant View, 10 miles north of Cortez. A longer, rougher route is State 146 three miles south of Cortez; dirt access roads from Aneth, Utah, and from State 47 between Blanding and Bluff may be impassable during wet weather.

At Square Tower Canyon there are interpretive displays and a 25-unit campground.

Aztec Ruins National Monument

The three-story, 500-room dwelling now set aside as Aztec Ruins National Monument was inhabited during two different periods by two different groups of people. The techniques used by the builders who constructed the complex more than 850 years ago along the Animas River (Rio de las Animas Perdidas—"River of Lost Souls") in northern New Mexico show the influence of the Chaco Canyon culture to the south. In the middle 1100's, only a short time after Aztec's completion, these people left. Then about 1225 the village was reoccupied, this time by a culture more similar to that of Mesa Verde to the north.

Aztec National Monument is just north of the town of Aztec off State Highway 550, 14 miles west of Farmington. It is open daily from 8 A.M. to 5 P.M. Admission is $1 per carload. At the visitor center you can examine artifacts from the classical Pueblo period.

A Great Kiva at the pueblo was restored in 1934, and the interior ceremonial setting has been recreated.

The final abandonment of Aztec had taken place by the end of the thirteenth century. The name "Aztec" is a misnomer; early settlers mistakenly associated the impressive structure with the great pyramids in Mexico.

CLIFF PALACE at Mesa Verde had eight floor levels and probably housed 200 people during its occupation in thirteenth century. Mesa Verde was one of the main centers of Anasazi culture.

Near the visitor center there is a small picnic area. There is no campground at the monument, but a public campground is maintained by the city of Aztec a mile south.

Chaco Canyon National Monument

The stillness of the deserted ruins of Chaco Canyon National Monument belies their history as one of the most important centers of commerce and culture in the prehistoric Southwest. A highly developed agricultural civilization reached its peak here in the eleventh and twelfth centuries.

A dozen large ruins and more than 300 smaller sites are preserved within the monument. To reach it from the north, turn off State Highway 44 at Blanco Trading Post and follow State Highway 56 for 23 miles to the monument's north entrance. The visitor center and museum is 7 miles beyond. (If you approach from the south, turn north on State 56 from U.S. 66 at Thoreau and drive 64 miles to the monument.) The monument is open from 8 A.M. to 5 P.M. daily; there is no admission fee.

Pueblo Bonito, Chettro Kettle, Casa Rinconada, and Pueblo del Arroyo are the largest ruins within the canyon. The ruins are open to visitors on a self-guided basis. Guide booklets to Pueblo Bonito and Casa Rinconada are available at the information station at each area; walking time for each tour is about an hour. During the summer, park rangers lead several tours of Pueblo Bonito and other ruins each day; during the winter there is a single tour of Pueblo Bonito at 1:30 P.M.

Chaco Canyon builders were expert masons; there are wall sections remaining in which the stones are so carefully fitted together that a knife blade can scarcely be inserted between them.

Most imposing of the structures within the monument is Pueblo Bonito, which covered over three acres of ground, contained 800 rooms, and may have housed 1,200 inhabitants at the peak of its development. Its D-shaped main building was terraced back from a one-story level around a central courtyard to four or five stories at the north wall. Construction began as early as 807 A.D. and continued for more than 300 years before the Chaco Canyon dwellings were abandoned beginning early in the twelfth century.

Thirty-two kivas were included in the Pueblo Bonito complex. The biggest kiva at Chaco Canyon, however, is the 64-foot-diameter ceremonial chamber of Casa Rinconada.

Chaco Canyon National Monument includes

PUEBLO BONITO is most impressive structure at Chaco Canyon, where Anasazi architecture reached peak. Stones are so carefully fitted that knife blade can scarcely be inserted between them.

the 58-unit Gallo Wash Campground a mile east of the visitor center.

Bandelier National Monument

While other centers of Pueblo culture were being abandoned by the end of the thirteenth century, the pueblo villages now preserved in Bandelier National Monument were just reaching their period of greatest development. Bandelier's cities probably were inhabited by Indians who had left the drought-plagued regions of Chaco Canyon, Aztec Ruins, and Mesa Verde.

The first of Bandelier's pueblos appeared late in the 1100's, and the transplanted civilization reached its greatest population and cultural development sometime between 1300 and 1500. However, drought, disease, and famine were the probable causes for the Pueblo people to once again seek new homes. The sites at Bandelier were abandoned by 1580. Descendants of the Bandelier residents are probably among the Rio Grande Valley's present-day Pueblo Indians.

Bandelier is located 46 miles northwest of Santa Fe via U.S. Highway 285 and State Highway 4 and 165 miles southeast of Aztec Ruins National Monument via State Highways 44, 126, and 4. The monument is open all year; the admission fee is $1 per carload per day.

The most accessible of Bandelier's ruins are in Frijoles Canyon. The Tyuonyi Ruin, less than a quarter mile from the visitor center, once contained 400 rooms and rose three stories tall. Other easily accessible ruins in the Frijoles Canyon complex include excavated kivas and cave rooms dug into the soft volcanic tuff that forms the canyon walls. A self-guided tour of the Frijoles Canyon ruins takes about one hour.

About 11 miles north of the visitor center is Tsankawi Ruin, an unexcavated structure that was two stories tall and contained more than 350 rooms. A three-mile round trip to the ruin from State Highway 4 follows an ancient Indian trail part of the way.

A museum is located at the visitor center, and nearby are a 100-unit campground, a picnic area, and overnight accommodations. During the summer, rangers conduct guided tours of the ruins and present slide programs and campfire lectures.

More than 60 miles of maintained trails within the monument offer access to the forested wilderness of Pajarito Plateau and the Jemez Mountains.

Pecos National Monument

Ruins of a pueblo village that was inhabited well into historic times are located at Pecos National

Monument, just off U.S. Highway 84-85 about 25 miles southeast of Santa Fe.

In the mid-1400's, Pecos pueblo was a multistoried dwelling of 660 rooms and at least 22 kivas. Its population of about 2,500 made it one of the largest and strongest pueblos in the area. In 1590 the pueblo was conquered by the Spaniard Castana de Sosa, but the pueblo's final decline came in the nineteenth century. Disease and enemy attacks reduced the once-great population to only 17 people by 1838. They left to join the Indians of Jemez pueblo across the Rio Grande.

A trail at the monument leads to the ruins of a mission church built about 1690, two pueblo structures, and a restored kiva. Archeologists have excavated much of the area.

A small museum and picnic facilities are located at the monument, which is open daily from 7 A.M. to 6 P.M.

TWO UTE INDIAN TRIBES

North of the modern-day Pueblo country and close to the center of ancient pueblo activity live the members of another Indian culture. The Ute Mountain and Southern Ute tribes occupy reservations in the southwest corner of Colorado and a small section of New Mexico.

Bands of Ute Indians once roamed across what is now Colorado, eastern Utah, and northern New Mexico. They were a hunting and gathering people whose range extended into the buffalo country of the Plains Indians after they acquired horses from the Spaniards. In the 1800's the Utes began losing land to settlers and miners; subsequent treaty agreements increasingly reduced their lands. Today Utes occupy a narrow strip along the Colorado-New Mexico border; a third Ute tribe—the 1,300 Northern Utes—lives on the Uintah and Ouray Reservation of northeastern Utah.

Originally the Ute strip along the Colorado border was a single reservation belonging to three Ute bands. In 1895, members of two of these bands agreed to accept individual land allotments. The third maintained its tribal ownership of land and was moved to 550,000 acres at the arid far western end of the strip; it became known as the Ute Mountain tribe. Homesteaders moved in among the other two bands, which eventually became the Southern Ute tribe. In the 1930's, the land which had not been homesteaded was returned to the Southern Utes, but of the 818,000

acres contained in the reservation's outer boundary, the Utes own only 305,000 acres.

Previously impoverished, the Utes in 1950 won a $31 million judgment from the United States government for land claims of the 1800's; the sum was divided among the three Ute tribes. Other tribal income has come from gas and oil discovered on the reservations. The principal source of individual income is farming and stock-raising.

The Ute Mountain and Southern Ute Indians speak the same Shoshonean dialect and have the same physical characteristics but are separately organized as tribes. Each is governed under a tribal constitution by an elected tribal council. Southern Ute tribal headquarters and the federal government's Southern Ute Agency are at Ignacio, Colorado; a tepee and a memorial to several Ute chiefs are located in Southern Ute Park on the agency grounds. Ute Mountain tribal headquarters and federal agency are at Towoac, Colorado.

Most of the 750 Southern Utes speak English and dress like the non-Indian neighbors who have lived among them since homesteading days. The Ute Mountain people have remained more isolated; the common language is the Ute tongue, and many of the women wear the traditional shawls or blankets. There are about 950 members in the tribe, most of whom live in or near Towoac; about 200 live near Blanding, Utah.

Though non-Indian ways are predominant today, two traditional ceremonies still are observed. Bear dances, social events held to welcome spring, take place in April or May. Sun dances, which are religious ceremonies, occur in July or August. Other events on the reservations include a tribal fair held each fall by the Southern Utes, including a parade, an arts and crafts display, and a queen contest.

Little craftwork is done now, although some beadwork and leatherwork is produced.

You can camp on the Southern Ute reservation at Lake Capote Campground, at the intersection of state highways 151 and 160. Permits may be obtained at a store located at the lake; the campground is open from May through September. Fishing is permitted on the Southern Ute reservation if you have a tribal permit, and hunting also is allowed. You may not fish or hunt on Ute Mountain land.

A motel-restaurant-museum complex is being planned for the Southern Ute reservation.

THE APACHES

White Mountain and San Carlos Tribes...Jicarillas...Mescaleros

Long after other tribes had been forced to give up the old ways, the Southwest's Apache Indians fought to preserve their land and their pattern of life. They were fierce warriors and amazingly hardy adversaries of both human foes and a harsh environment.

Some historians say the name *Apache* comes from a Zuni word for "enemy," while others contend it is from a Ute name or a Yavapai word meaning "the people." Tales of Apache raiding parties and years of bitter warfare with the U.S. Army made the name so well known that when many people said "Indian" they meant "Apache."

The drive that once produced successful Apache warriors today makes the tribe among the most progressive of Indians. In just two generations, against overwhelming odds, they adjusted to an alien economy and new ways of living. Their development of natural resources and outdoor recreation potential, along with their ability as stockmen, has made them more prosperous than many other tribes.

Some 12,000 Apaches live on four reservations in Arizona and New Mexico. The "Western Apaches" of adjacent San Carlos and Fort Apache reservations in Arizona are more similar to their Navajo cousins than are the Jicarillas and the Mescaleros of New Mexico. The New Mexico Apaches adopted more traits from Plains Indians in neighboring territories.

RODEO TIME is exciting at Whiteriver on Fort Apache reservation. This is cattle country, and rodeos are popular events on all four Apache reservations.

As you travel through Apache country today, the pickup truck is a more common sight than the horse, and frame houses have largely replaced the brush wickiups which once served as temporary houses for a people on the move. Young people and many older ones have adopted modern dress, although many women still prefer to wear the traditional long full skirts and loose "Mother Hubbard" blouses.

Many people still speak the Athabaskan language. And the very youngest Apaches perpetuate one custom—babies are still placed on cradle boards to sleep or to ride along on their mothers' backs.

Nomadic hunters from the North

The Apaches are descendants of Athabaskan bands who came from the North after other Indian cultures were already well established in the Southwest. Just when they arrived is not known, but they were here by the time the Spaniards came in the mid-sixteenth century. Different bands developed different cultural traits as they roamed from what is now southern Colorado down into Mexico and from Arizona as far east as Oklahoma, hunting and raiding. The Apaches quickly capitalized on the introduction of horses to the Southwest by the Spaniards, and their ability to strike quickly and effectively increased accordingly.

After the United States acquired the area from Mexico, more settlers moved into Apache territory—and more Apache raids followed. Four decades of warfare marked by cruelty and misunderstandings on both sides did not end until 1886, when Geronimo and his band of Chiricahua Apaches finally surrendered.

Ceremonials and special events

Among the most important Apache ceremonies are the "coming out" observances for young girls. During these ceremonies the dramatic mountain spirits dance (sometimes called crown dance) is performed around a fire at night. Wearing headdresses of colorfully painted strips of wood and black cloths that cover their faces, the dancers represent friendly spirits who live in mountain caves and beneath the horizon. Parts of this dance also can be seen at Gallup's Inter-Tribal Indian Ceremonial and Flagstaff's All-Indian Pow Wow.

Other Apache religious ceremonies are simpler. In addition, rodeos and fairs are held in various communities throughout the summer. Many of the Apache ceremonials are scheduled only a short time ahead, but you can obtain information about them by inquiring at the tribal offices of reservations through which you travel.

Apache crafts

When the Apaches were a nomadic people who needed lightweight, unbreakable carrying utensils, they produced beautiful coiled storage baskets and bowls. Some of these fine baskets can be seen in museums throughout the Southwest, but for the most part the art of weaving them is dying out. Limited quantities of basketry, beadwork, and leatherwork are made by a few craftsmen.

FORT APACHE INDIAN RESERVATION

In the beautiful White Mountains of east-central Arizona, the 1,664,872-acre Fort Apache Indian Reservation is being developed as a major recreation area by the White Mountain Apache Tribe. The building of new access roads, 26 mountain lakes, and hundreds of campsites shows that the tribe is serious about the motto it has adopted—*Hon-Dah,* Apache for "be my guest."

The recreation business is a relatively recent undertaking for the tribe. Progressive leaders of this formerly isolated people recommended it as a means of promoting economic independence, and the White Mountain Recreation Enterprise was formed in 1954. Since then, millions of dollars of tribal funds have been used to build lakes,

TRADING POST is place to shop for everything from flour to bridles to children's red wagons. This one is at Whiteriver on Fort Apache Reservation.

tourist accommodations, and other facilities; care has been taken to preserve the area's primitive atmosphere. A sports complex near Sunrise Lake is being planned as the largest winter resort in Arizona.

Much of the reservation's southern boundary is formed by the Black River, which separates it from the San Carlos Indian Reservation. Originally part of a single large reservation established in the early 1870's, the Fort Apache and San Carlos reservations were separated in 1897. More than 5,000 Indians live on the Fort Apache Reservation.

Climate and scenery on the reservation ranges from the semi-desert setting of its southwest corner to the forested mountains in the northeast. The famed Mogollon Rim marks part of the reservation's northern border and the edge of the high plateau country beyond.

Long before the White Mountain Apaches began their recreation enterprise, the cattle industry was important to them. More than 20,000 head of cattle graze on the reservation, and if you're here in September you may see some of the long cattle drives that precede October cattle auctions at Whiteriver, McNary, and Apache Springs. The reservation also includes commercial timberland; the tribe operates a large sawmill at Whiteriver.

While you are on the reservation you can explore ruins of prehistoric dwellings that predate the Apaches' presence here. Ask directions for getting to some of them from Whiteriver, the tribal capital. Hundreds of ruins scattered across the reservation include fairly elaborate cliff dwellings as well as simple improvements on caves. Only a few of the ruins are excavated. You must not dig at any site or deface or disturb any ruins, but otherwise you are free to explore as you

Salt and Black Rivers are dividing line between Fort Apache and San Carlos Indian Reservations.

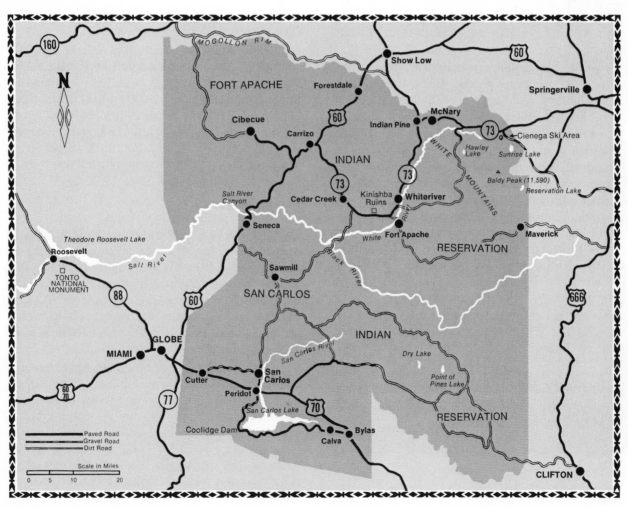

BRUSH WICKIUPS—often supplemented with boards, canvas, or scrap metal—still can be seen but have been mostly replaced by frame houses. Settlement of Cibecue has many wickiup dwellings.

wish. You may pick up arrowheads found on the surface.

You can buy supplies or just browse in trading posts at Whiteriver, Cibecue, Cedar Creek, Eastfork, McNary, and Carrizo. Beadwork and other crafts are on display and for sale at a shop in Whiteriver.

Starting with the Cedar Creek Pow Wow in June, Indian ceremonials, rodeos, and other celebrations are held almost every weekend throughout the summer. Visitors are welcome, and you may take photographs. Dates usually are set only a few months or weeks in advance, but you can obtain information and directions by stopping at the tribal offices in Whiteriver. The Tribal Fair and Rodeo in Whiteriver (see page 61) is always held during the Labor Day weekend.

For further information and a recreation map, write to the White Mountain Recreation Enterprise, P.O. Box 218, Whiteriver, Arizona 85941.

Salt River Canyon gateway

The southern gateway to the Fort Apache Reservation is the spectacular Salt River Canyon. As you drive onto the reservation on U.S. Highway 60 from Globe, the mountains give way abruptly to a majestic, colorful chasm. The highway drops down to cross the river on a low-level bridge,

then climbs to the opposite rim.

Farther into the reservation, take a side trip west to Cibecue if you would like to visit an Indian settlement that has been little changed by time. Then return to U.S. 60 and turn onto State Highway 73 at the Carrizo Junction for a trip through red mountains and dark green junipers to some extensive prehistoric ruins, an old Army fort, and the tribal capital of Whiteriver.

Kinishba Ruins

The apartment-house dwellings now known as Kinishba may have housed as many as 2,000 people at the peak of their occupation in the late 1200's. Now a national historic landmark, the remnants of this settlement from pre-Apache days are located 8 miles southwest of Whiteriver. (You take a dirt road off State 73 for about a mile.) Visitors are welcome the year around.

The name Kinishba comes from Apache words combined to mean "brown house." The village contained 400 to 500 rooms in two large apartment houses and several smaller outlying buildings. Some of the rooms have been reconstructed by archeology students from the University of Arizona. The ruins are presently fenced off while restabilization work is being done, but you can still get good views of them.

BABY wrapped in soft cloths rides in cradleboard on mother's back.

KINISHBA may have housed 2,000 people in late 1200's, was abandoned after 1350. The ruins are now a national historic landmark.

Fort Apache

Strategically located between Apache and Navajo territory, Fort Apache once was an important Army post for campaigns against such Apache warriors as Geronimo and Nachez. The fort is just east of the Fort Apache Junction, 4 miles south of Whiteriver.

Since 1924 the fort has been used as an Indian school. Many of the original buildings are still standing, and visitors are welcome.

Established in 1870 as Camp Ord, the fort later was renamed "Fort Apache" in honor of the Apache chief Cochise, who visited here.

Whiteriver, the tribal capital

Four miles north of the Fort Apache junction is the town of Whiteriver, where the White Mountain tribal headquarters are located. Here also are the tribally-operated sawmill and trading posts full of interesting merchandise.

A festive atmosphere settles over the community for the three days preceding Labor Day, when bronc riders and crown dancers perform at the White Mountain Apache Tribal Fair. The Apache sunrise dance, recognizing the "coming out" of teen-aged Apache girls, is a highlight of the fair.

Two fish hatcheries

North of Whiteriver you can visit a trout hatchery that supplies several million rainbow trout each year. To reach the Alchesay National Fish Hatchery, named for an Apache chief, you turn off State 73 about 5 miles north of Whiteriver, then drive 3 miles up Whiteriver Canyon. Farther north off State 73 is the Williams Creek National Fish Hatchery, the oldest federal fish hatchery in the state. Visitors are welcome at both hatcheries from 8 A.M. until 5 P.M.

McNary and the Scenic Railroad

In the logging town of McNary, a non-reservation enclave, you can board a coach on Arizona's only remaining steam-powered railroad line for a 40-mile trip through some of the most attractive country in the state. The White Mountain Scenic Railroad (not operated by the tribe) climbs from Ponderosa pine forest around McNary to aspen-fringed meadows at Apache Springs, then returns.

The 5½-hour run starts daily except Sunday at 9:30 A.M., Memorial Day until Labor Day. Tickets are $5.95 for adults, $3.95 ages 3 to 12, free under age 3. For reservations, write to the White Mountain Scenic Railroad, Box 496, McNary, Arizona 85930.

Recreation lakes

One of the reservation's most popular recreation areas is Hawley Lake, 18 miles southeast of McNary in a forest of fir, spruce, pine, and aspen. Around its 7½-mile shoreline are 100 campsites; rental cabins and summer homes; a large dock with rental boats; and a store and service station. Sailboating is popular here, and you can swim at designated areas. Formed by a dam built in 1957, Hawley is the reservation's third largest lake.

Farther east is the recently-completed Sunrise Lake, largest on the reservation. Extensive development is planned for this area. Next in size is Reservation Lake, with campground and boat launching areas. Gasoline-powered motor boats may not be used on any of the reservation lakes, but electric trolling motors are permitted.

Hunting and fishing

Game that can be hunted by non-Indians includes antelope, elk, bear, javelina, waterfowl, dove, band-tail pigeons, grouse, quail, predators, rabbit, and squirrel. Guides are not required, but the White Mountain Recreation Enterprise can recommend a guide service if you want one.

Twenty-six mountain lakes, hundreds of small ponds, and 300 miles of streams full of rainbow, brown, brook, and Apache native trout should leave no fisherman disappointed. Nearly half of Arizona's trout waters are on the Fort Apache Reservation, and there are bass, bluegill, and catfish in some of the warm waters. Hawley Lake, with its all-weather access road, has become popular for ice-fishing.

Hunters must have an Arizona license and a reservation hunting permit; fishermen need an Arizona fishing license, an Arizona trout stamp, and a reservation fishing permit. These can be obtained from license dealers throughout the state.

Camping

Eight hundred camping and picnic sites have been established on the reservation, ranging from large campgrounds with piped water to remote single units.

You need a camping permit, which can be purchased wherever fishing permits are sold. Permits are 75 cents a day per vehicle; $5 for an annual permit entitling you to camp up to 10 days in any one place; and $30 for a season permit to remain in one location all summer. Fees are used to build and maintain campgrounds.

SAN CARLOS INDIAN RESERVATION

Tan mesas and rolling rangeland, arid valleys and forested mountains make up the San Carlos Indian Reservation. You drive from mesquite and cactus-dotted desert terrain in the southern part into stands of pine, oak, and juniper in the high country farther north. There are other contrasts, too. Here as in much of the Southwest's Indian country you can explore primitive Indian ruins, many unmapped and seldom seen, or visit modern structures—such as giant Coolidge Dam.

The cattle industry is the main source of income for the 4,700 San Carlos Apaches, and much of the 1,877,216-acre reservation is grazing land. Mining, lumbering, railroading, and agriculture also provide jobs on and near the reservation. The tribe is becoming more active in developing the recreational potential of the area to attract visitors to its unspoiled scenery and fine outdoor sports opportunities. Recreation information and dates of special events can be obtained from the San Carlos Tribe, San Carlos, Arizona 85550.

To visit the reservation, drive east on U.S. Highway 70 from Globe, just off the reservation. Easily accessible from Globe are the ruins of Tonto National Monument (see page 73), and while you are in Globe you can visit the ruins of the prehistoric pueblo Indian site of Besh-Ba-Gowah.

Besh-Ba-Gowah

On the outskirts of Globe is the ancient Salado Indian site of Besh-Ba-Gowah, which contained about 200 rooms during its active period, about 1225 to 1400 A.D. Situated on a bluff above Pinal Creek, the ruins include some two dozen roofless rooms clearly defined by stone walls. You may roam where you wish throughout the 2-acre site, which is open at all hours.

To reach Besh-Ba-Gowah ("metal camp"), follow Broad Street about a mile south of the center of Globe, then cross the second bridge over Pinal Creek and go half a mile to the marked access road on your right. The Globe Community Center, adjacent to the ruins, has swimming pool and picnic facilities.

A small collection of bows, tools, and pottery from the ruins is on display in Globe's city hall, West Cedar and North Pine. The city hall is open Monday through Friday from 8 A.M. to 5 P.M.

Coolidge Dam

Coolidge Dam, a 250-foot structure which impounds the waters of the Gila River, was completed in 1930 to provide irrigation water and electric power for the Upper Gila Valley. The dam's reservoir, San Carlos Lake, is one of the largest lakes in Arizona.

You reach Coolidge Dam by turning south at the junction of U.S. 70 and State 170 onto Indian Service Route 3 (a few miles of gravel).

The reservoir covered one of the ancient burial grounds of the Apaches. A concrete slab on the lake floor protects the graves, since the Indians considered it a desecration to move them.

Desert terrain surrounds the lake, a center for fishing, swimming, water-skiing, and boating. The San Carlos Apaches have developed 18 campgrounds around the lake; signs mark their locations. The Apache Bait and Tackle near the dam can provide information as well as supplies.

North to San Carlos

From Coolidge Dam you return to the junction with U.S. 70 on your way to the reservation's capital town, San Carlos. You pass through Peridot, named for a semi-precious stone rather resembling an emerald when cut and mounted; many have been found near here, as have smoky topazes. If you're a rockhound you may want to do some searching in this area. Be sure to get permission first at the tribal office at San Carlos.

North of Peridot, State 170—about 4 miles of paved road—takes you past farming plots and cattle corrals to San Carlos. A town of lawns and shade trees, San Carlos is the reservation's main trading center and the seat of the 11-member tribal council. If by luck your visit falls on the right day, you can see one of the periodic tribal rodeos or a ceremonial dance. Inquire at the tribal office or the government's San Carlos Agency to find out about activities that may take place during your visit.

From San Carlos you can continue northwest, on a graded road, to the Sawmill Road junction, then turn left and drive 16 miles to U.S. 60 near

SAN CARLOS Reservoir, formed by Coolidge Dam, is a popular recreation area for water sports, camping.

Seneca, 35 miles from Globe. Or you can drive 13 miles west over gravel and paved roads to Cutter, a few miles east of Globe. Either route will provide fine views of distant mesas—yellow and tan rimmed with blue and purple shadows—that are typical of the reservation and worth the trip in themselves. Check locally on road conditions. The all-paved alternative is back over State 170 and U.S. 70, via Peridot.

Hunting and fishing

Big game hunting and excellent fishing make sportsmen among the most enthusiastic visitors to the San Carlos Reservation. Permits for deer, elk, bear, and javelina are offered by the tribe. Small game includes quail and waterfowl.

San Carlos Lake provides excellent bass fishing. This is the only place where no reservation fishing permit is required, and the season lasts all year. Other lakes and streams across the reservation are well stocked with bass and trout, and the tribe has been building and improving more waters. One of the most recently developed areas is Point of Pines Lake, more than 30 acres of trout waters in the east-central part of the reservation. There is a campground here. Another of the larger lakes is nearby Dry Lake, and about a hundred smaller ponds dot the reservation.

Permits for hunting and fishing can be obtained at the tribal office in San Carlos or from license dealers around the state.

Camping

Many improved campsites have been completed by the San Carlos Apaches, among them the 18 camping areas at San Carlos Lake. Cassadore Springs, 16 miles north of San Carlos, is another good location to camp. If you want to get among the pines, follow the same road another 5 miles to Hilltip; this area is rugged and colorful, with good campsites and a plentiful water supply.

To camp on the reservation you will need a recreation permit, which costs $1 per day or $5 per season per vehicle. Permits can be picked up at the tribal office or from dealers who sell hunting and fishing permits.

JICARILLA APACHE RESERVATION

A meandering strip of land in the mountain country of northwestern New Mexico is home for some 1,800 members of the Jicarilla Apache Tribe. Abundant wildlife and trout-stocked waters make the 742,315-acre Jicarilla Indian Reservation an attractive destination for hunters, fishermen, and campers.

The reservation was established in two parts, the northern half in 1887 and the southern half in 1908. Mountains, deep canyons, and wide valleys set the northern section apart from the open plains and rolling hills, sandstone bluffs and mesa canyons of the southern part.

The Jicarillas have an economy based on natural resources, tourism, and livestock raising. The name *Jicarilla* comes from a Spanish word meaning "little basket," for basketry is a native craft of the tribe. Unfortunately, this art has almost died out. In 1962 the tribe started an arts and crafts program to regenerate interest in crafts, and some basket weaving, beadwork, and leatherwork are being done.

Many of the traditional aspects of the Jicarilla way of life have disappeared, and ceremonial occasions have lost much of their original meaning. The annual Stone Lake Fiesta held September 14, 15, and 16, originally to signify the reunion of the two divisions of the tribe, is open to the public. A night of dances is followed by a day of races between the White and Red clans, as well as a rodeo and another night of dances. There is no admission charge.

For details about ceremonies and for other information, write to the Jicarilla Apache Tribe (Department of Tourism and Outdoor Recreation, P.O. Box 384, Dulce, New Mexico 87528) or inquire at the tribal office when you are on the reservation.

Dulce, the Jicarilla capital

At the northern tip of the reservation the tribal government has its headquarters at Dulce. Here also is a Jicarilla Arts and Crafts Retail Shop, and several Apache artists exhibit in Dulce. In July the town is the scene of competition among Jicarilla cowboys at the Little Beaver Round-up.

A motel and a restaurant are located here. A narrow gauge railroad runs through town, then along the Navajo River and into Colorado.

If you'd like to explore some prehistoric Indian ruins in the back country, check in Dulce or at the Department of Tourism Field Office at Stone Lake for directions for getting to them.

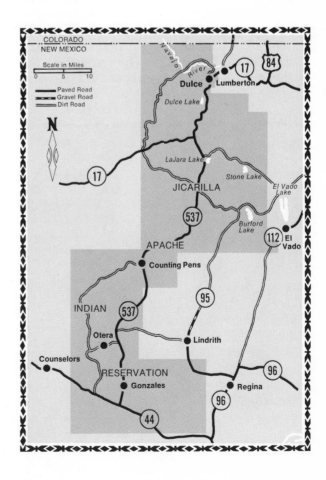

JICARILLA Apaches perform tribal dance. Tepees (these are made of canvas) show influence of Plains Indians; members of tribe live in them during annual Stone Lake Fiesta.

Recreation lakes

Five miles south of Dulce is picturesque Dulce Lake. You will find camping facilities and a boat launching pad and dock here. Farther south on State Highway 537 is LaJara Lake, which also has a camping area.

A graded road east of LaJara Lake leads to Stone Lake, a natural body of melted ice with 5½ miles of shoreline. Fishing and boating supplies are available at a lakeside store operated by the tribe. The north shore of the lake is considered sacred ground by the Apaches.

Hunting and fishing

The Jicarilla tribe points out that its reservation is one of the best pasturelands in the world for mule deer. In addition to big-game hunting, the reservation offers year-round trout fishing in its lakes and streams. The Navajo River crosses the northeast corner of the reservation for 13 miles.

Reservation hunting and fishing permits are issued by the Tribal Game and Fish Department. For information, write to the Jicarilla Apache Tribe, Department of Game and Fish, P.O. Box

147, Dulce, New Mexico 87528. Guide services are available, but since they are limited it is wise to make arrangements ahead.

Camping

There are several campgrounds in the northern part of the reservation but none in the southern half. However, you can camp anywhere except within 300 yards of stock watering places unless posted otherwise. Water is available from windmills and springs. Camping permits can be obtained at tribal headquarters in Dulce, at the Stone Lake store, or from wardens who patrol the campgrounds and lakes.

MESCALERO INDIAN RESERVATION

Operating a ski resort is one way in which the Mescalero Apaches of southern New Mexico utilize the natural resources of their 460,000-acre reservation. Camping, hunting, fishing, and other outdoor sports facilities also are being developed by the tribe.

Named by the Spanish for the mescal cactus they used for food, drink, and fiber, the Mescalero Apaches occupied the location of their present reservation when the Spaniards entered Indian country in the mid-1500's. The reservation was established in 1873. Today about 2,000 Apaches live here.

Timber provides the tribe's chief income. The Mescaleros also raise cattle, do wage work on and off the reservation, and run tribal enterprises such as the Apache Summit Lodge, a hunting and fishing headquarters on U.S. 70 midway through the reservation (cabins, a restaurant, and an Indian crafts store are located here).

For further information about the reservation, write to the Mescalero Apache Tribe, P.O. Box 176, Mescalero, New Mexico 88340.

The village of Mescalero

Tribal offices are located at the Community Center in Mescalero, on U.S. 70 in the western part of the reservation. The tribe is governed under a constitution by the 8-member elected Tribal Business Committee.

Mescalero also is where the annual coming-of-age ceremonial for young girls takes place each year from July 1 to 4. The event includes the dance of the mountain spirits, wearing the dramatic crown headdresses. The girls in the ceremony do dances in a specially constructed large tepee; on the fourth day, they take part in a foot race while the tepee is taken down. During the four days of the colorful ceremonial, such events as dances by visiting tribes, a rodeo, and games and races for children also are scheduled. Admission to the rodeo and ceremonials is $1 for adults, 50 cents for children.

Just below the village of Mescalero is the Mescalero National Fish Hatchery, which stocks waters on the reservation each week. Visitors are welcome from 7:30 A.M. to 4 P.M. daily.

Sierra Blanca Ski Resort

On the north ridge of Sierra Blanca Peak, the highest point on the reservation at 12,003 feet, the Sierra Blanca Ski Resort is operated by the Mescalero tribe. A lodge, restaurant, ski shop, and rental facilities are located here.

Hunting and fishing

Deer and bear hunts on the reservation are open to the public. A state big game hunting license and a tribal permit are required, and all hunters must first check in at the Mescalero Community Center. Rental horses and guide services are available; contact the tribal office at Mescalero for information.

Fishing is permitted at Eagle Creek Lakes Recreation Area, about three miles west of the Alto post office; Ruidoso Recreation Area above Ruidoso; and Cienegita Lakes, south of Ruidoso Recreation Area. Along with native German brown and cutthroat trout, waters are stocked with rainbow. The season lasts from about mid-May to mid-September. You need a reservation fishing permit (obtainable at the fishing area gates or at the tribal office) along with a New Mexico license.

Camping

You can camp at Ruidoso Recreation Area, Eagle Lakes Recreation Area, and Apache Summit campgrounds for $2 per car per night. Picnicking fee for reservation recreation areas is $1 per car per day.

BREAD-MAKING, INDIAN STYLE

Three distinctive breads made by Indians in the Southwest are the interestingly shaped loaves of the Pueblos, the thin-layered cornmeal *piki* of the Hopis, and the flat round frybread of the Navajos and Apaches.

Lop-eared loaves of bread baked in high-domed outdoor ovens are traditional with New Mexico's Pueblo Indians. The bread is simply a basic white loaf, but the shape is unique. Usually the loaf is divided into three sections, though there are differences among various villages; the Zunis, for instance, divide it into four lobes. On baking day a fire is built in the clay oven, the coals are raked aside, the bread is put in, and the door is sealed. Loaves of this bread are made for village festivals, so the day before such an occasion is a good time to visit the pueblo to see the baking process.

The making of piki is a centuries-old custom with the Hopis. Water is added to the finely ground flour of blue Indian corn to make a soupy batter. The breadmaker dips her hand in the batter and deftly smears a tissue-thin layer across a hot stone griddle. In seconds it bakes into a translucent blue sheet, which is gently lifted from the griddle while a second smear of batter is wiped quickly across the hot stone. As this bakes, the first sheet is placed on top of it; then the two are lifted from the griddle and folded into an elongated, multilayered roll. The warm piki, crisp yet tender, is rich with the flavor of corn. Some cooks add a pinch of powdered chiles to the batter.

Navajo or Apache frybread is made from a biscuit-type dough which is divided into balls and flattened between the palms of the hand. The cook dexterously flips the piece of dough from hand to hand, patting and stretching it into a circle about 6 or 8 inches across. Then she fries it golden brown and puffy in deep fat and serves it hot.

PUEBLO BREAD

PIKI BREAD

FRYBREAD

THE PIMAS & THE PAPAGOS

'River People' Near Phoenix...Southern Arizona 'Desert People'

Two thousand years ago a peaceful agricultural people now called the Hohokam lived in the desert country of southern Arizona. Today the land they once cultivated is being farmed by Indian tribes who may be their descendants—the Pima "River People" and the Papago "Desert People." Some 7,500 Pima Indians live on reservations just outside Phoenix; farther south, 5,000 Papagos occupy land stretching from Mexico more than halfway to Phoenix and from Tucson's outskirts almost halfway to the California border.

The prehistoric Hohokam Indians had built a system of irrigation canals in the Salt and Gila river valleys by 700 A.D. Over the following centuries they enlarged it until there were 200 miles of ditches—a remarkable achievement, since they had only the crudest of tools. Excellent pottery and large, adobe-walled ball courts were among other Hohokam accomplishments. Actually, less is known about the Hohokam than about some other early Southwest cultures because they cremated their dead and because the wood used in their houses cannot be dated by the tree-ring method.

After the thirteenth century, pueblo-dwelling Salado people (named from the Spanish word for "salty" because of the Salt River) moved into the area from farther north. Multistoried houses were built along with the single-room earth and brush structures of the Hohokam. Several ruins from this period have been excavated and are open to the public (see page 73).

Though they lived side by side, the Hohokam and the Salado apparently maintained their own separate cultural traits. Then about 1400 the Salado left, possibly because of raids by warlike Indians. It is not known whether the Hohokam stayed or moved south to where another Hohokam group had been living without penetration by the Salado. When the Spaniards arrived in the sixteenth century the Papago Indians occupied this southern region, and the Pimas were established in the Gila River basin.

Spanish missionaries came in the sixteenth century, but the first European whose influence had a deep effect on the Indian way of life was missionary-explorer Father Eusebio Kino, late in the next century. He brought cattle and horses to the Indians he found farming the desert region of southern Arizona and Mexico. Besides the missionaries, there was little outside contact during the years Spain and then Mexico claimed jurisdiction over the Indians. Then in the mid-1800's the United States acquired the area, and ranchers began appropriating land and diverting water for their own uses. In 1859 the first reservation was created for the Pimas, but not until 1874 was any land secured for the Papagos. Over the following decades reservation lands were increased to their present sizes.

Today, as in ancient times, agriculture is basic to the economy of both the Pimas and the Papagos. However, their incomes are among the lowest of all the tribes in Arizona, and many people

PAPAGO INDIANS like these children have attended whitewashed church on San Xavier reservation since 1797. Church is called 'White Dove of the Desert.'

leave the reservations to seek work. Much of the reservation land near Phoenix is leased to non-Indian farmers.

The Pimas, living on the outskirts of a major urban area, have become acculturated to a large extent. Almost all speak English. Among the Papagos, too, non-Indian ways have been accepted to a greater extent than among some other tribes. Still, a visit to these reservations will be enjoyed by the person interested in the continuing story of Indian life. While you are here you can see the work of Indian craftsmen, visit archeological diggings, and enjoy the desert scenery. Late winter and early spring, when the desert flowers are in bloom, are particularly good times to travel through this country. There are no restrictions on visiting the reservations, other than those of common courtesy.

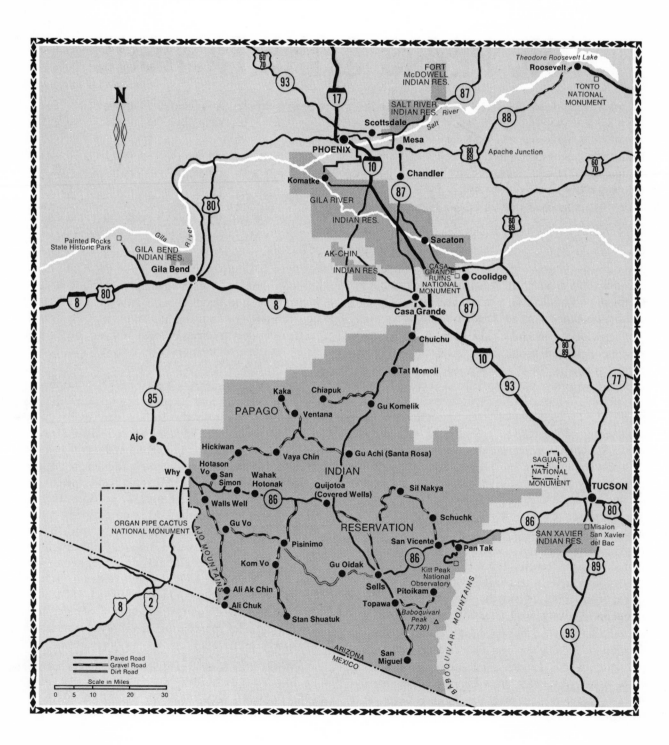

Papago and Pima crafts

Papagos produce more basketry for commercial trade than any other North American tribe. In recent years basket-making has been encouraged by a tribal arts and crafts program which sponsors a shop in Sells. Papago work also can be purchased on the reservation at Kitt Peak National Observatory and at the six licensed trading posts, at the gift shop of Mission San Xavier del Bac, and in the larger cities in Arizona.

Some of the finest examples of Indian basketry ever produced are the closely coiled baskets once made in quantity by the Pima Indians. Unfortunately, very few Pimas are making baskets now. Miniature baskets once woven by the Pimas are particularly interesting. These tiny pieces—some less than a half inch across—were made in intricate detail, following the same shapes and geometric designs used for regular-sized baskets. You can see examples of Pima baskets in museums.

A small amount of polished red pottery is made by Maricopa Indians who live on the Gila River and Salt River reservations. Heavy pottery, sometimes decorated in black, is produced in very limited amounts by the Papagos.

PHOENIX

A good starting point for visiting the Pima and Papago reservations is Arizona's capital city, Phoenix. While you are here, you can visit an excellent Indian museum and a large Indian school. Pueblo Grande, a thirteenth century village ruin, also is in Phoenix (see page 73). A variety of Indian craftwork can be found in shops in Phoenix and Scottsdale.

The Heard Museum

A graceful Spanish Colonial-style building at 22 East Monte Vista Road houses one of the finest Indian museums in the Southwest—the Heard Museum of Anthropology and Primitive Arts. The museum has an extensive collection of Hopi artifacts including a colorful Kachina Gallery of more than 450 dolls; a Navajo rug room and a pottery room with examples from different Southwest Indian groups; and a gallery of Indian paintings with a different Indian artist exhibiting each month. Exhibits describe prehistoric Southwest cultures and Plains, South American, and Northwest tribes.

PAINTINGS by Indian artists capture attention of young visitors to Heard Museum. Painting has become an important twentieth-century Indian art form.

THE CHOICES IN PAPAGO BASKETRY

Subtle natural colors which mellow evenly and imperceptibly over the years are used in the coiled baskets made by the Papago Indians.

Papago baskets are made of stiff filler held in place by a wrapping fiber, a technique which lends itself to circular work. Rectangular pieces are rare. Often the filler is exposed, by a method sometimes called "lazy squaw" because it involves less work. Now "open-stitch" is replacing this term; "split-stitch" describes its intricate forms. Bear grass, a light gray-green that browns when fully dry, is the most common filler.

The most common binding fiber comes from yucca stalk, sun-bleached to a dull white. Another white fiber comes from willow stalk, recognizable by its slight sheen. Black comes from the seed pod of the devil's claw weed, avocado green from natural unbleached yucca leaf, and rare red from yucca root.

Quality of design and fineness of stitch determine price, and pieces that at first glance look similar actually may vary quite a lot. Inspect for firmness and evenness before buying—some hasty open-stitch work will dry and loosen with time.

You will find a wide range of articles to choose from. Covered baskets and animal forms in baskets or toy figures are Papago specialties, and plaques, trays, and small dish-type baskets are very popular, too. Some recent directions include a kind of open-work adornment on conventional baskets and adaptations for women's handbags.

ARRAY OF PAPAGO BASKETRY includes both coiled work with geometric designs and open-stitch pieces with exposed filler. Only natural colors are used. Rectangular basket is rare.

Early in April the museum hosts a two-day Indian Fair in which a dozen different tribes may be represented. The entire museum is turned into a fairground, and Indian craftsmen demonstrate their skills (all craft articles are for sale). A platform and bleachers are set up for dances scheduled throughout each day.

Also sponsored by the museum are shows by the Navajo Arts and Crafts Guild and the Hopi Arts and Crafts-Silvercraft Cooperative Guild, held separately sometime during the winter, each for about two weeks. A weaver and a silversmith from the Navajo Guild work all day demonstrating their crafts, and a potter, a silversmith, and a weaver do the same during the Hopi show.

The Heard museum is open from 10 A.M. to 5 P.M. Monday through Saturday, 1 to 5 P.M. Sunday. Admission is 50 cents for adults, 25 cents for students.

Phoenix Indian School

Students from 20 different tribes attend the Phoenix Indian School, one of the Southwest's oldest and largest Indian boarding schools. The majority of students—in all there are more than 1,000—come from the Hopi, Papago, Navajo, Pima, Apache, and Colorado River reservations.

The campus is at North Central Avenue and Indian School Road. Student guides conduct tours of the school each Friday, from 9 to 11 A.M. and 1 to 3 P.M., September through May. An annual spring open house includes an arts and crafts exhibit, performances by Indian dancers and school music groups, and workshops in which you may observe class routine.

The school was established in 1891 and is run by the Bureau of Indian Affairs. Students must be at least one quarter Indian; nearly all are full-blooded. Curriculum includes vocational as well as academic subjects, for grades 7 through 12.

THREE PREHISTORIC RUINS

Ruins from the prehistoric Hohokam-Salado period can be visited at three different sites within easy reach of Phoenix and the Pima and Papago reservations.

Pueblo Grande

Remains of a Hohokam village and irrigation canals which were in use from about 1200 to 1400 can be viewed at Pueblo Grande, 4619 E. Washington Street in Phoenix. A guide-yourself tour leaflet can be picked up at the Pueblo Grande Museum, where artifacts from the ruins are on display.

The museum is open from 9 A.M. to 5 P.M. weekdays and 1 P.M. to 5 P.M. Sundays (closed Saturdays and major holidays). Admission is free.

Tonto National Monument

Cliff dwellings occupied by Salado Indians more than 600 years ago are preserved as Tonto National Monument.

To reach the monument from Phoenix, take U.S. Highway 60-70 to Apache Junction; turn left on State Highway 88 and follow the Apache Trail three miles beyond Roosevelt. If you start at Globe, drive 28 miles northwest on State 88 (see map on page 59). A federal entrance fee of $1 per carload is charged at the monument.

The two main sections of the ruins were built in natural caves that have protected them from wind and rain. Lower Ruin has 19 rooms, and Upper Ruin—about a mile away—has 40. A $1/2$-mile guide-yourself trail leads to Lower Ruin; to visit Upper Ruin you must make arrangements at least four days ahead.

Begin at the visitor center, where artifacts and plant remains recovered from the ruins tell the story of Salado life. Visitors unable to make the climb to the ruins can view a 10-minute slide-sound program about the dwelling.

Casa Grande

Midway between Phoenix and Tucson stand the ruins of six prehistoric Hohokam villages which have been partially excavated within the boundaries of Casa Grande Ruins National Monument. Take State Highway 87 to the monument, which is a mile north of Coolidge. (The monument is not at the town of Casa Grande.)

Casa Grande itself is a four-story building which dominates the village in which it was built and commands a view of the other village ruins. Built to last in about 1350 with thick earth walls and deep foundations, it was nevertheless abandoned by 1450 as the Indians of the Gila Valley left this type of village.

The first European to report seeing Casa Grande was Father Kino, who found it in ruin in 1694.

THICK WALLS of Casa Grande rose four stories above desert floor, are now protected from rain by a roof. Indians built Casa Grande during fourteenth century.

He gave it the present name—Spanish for "big house."

You can see the Casa Grande ruins from 7 A.M. to 6 P.M. daily. The federal fee system is in effect at the monument. Stop first at the visitor center, where Hohokam artifacts are displayed. Guided tours are scheduled hourly on the quarter hour, 9:15 A.M. to 4:15 P.M.; or you can follow a guide-yourself trail.

INDIAN RESERVATIONS AROUND PHOENIX

The suburbs of Phoenix crowd right up to the boundaries of several Indian reservations, so you can see cattle grazing and tractors plowing on Indian land against the backdrop of a modern metropolis. Not colorful tourist destinations like some other Indian lands, these valley reservations are occupied by tribes whose native culture has largely disappeared.

The Pimas are the largest Indian group living here, but there also are Maricopas, Yavapais, and a few Apaches. The Pimas live primarily on the Gila River reservation south of Phoenix, and they share it and the Salt River reservation with a smaller group of Maricopas. The Maricopas are a Yuman-speaking group that migrated from the Colorado River area before the Spaniards arrived. Another Yuman tribe, the Yavapai, lives on the Fort McDowell reservation north of Phoenix. (Other Yavapai Indians live on small reservations near Prescott). The Maricopa-Ak-Chin reservation south of Phoenix is shared by Papago and Pima Indians.

Gila River Indian Reservation

South of Phoenix on the Gila River Indian Reservation you can view Indian petroglyphs, visit a mission school, and stop at the government's Pima Agency in Sacaton to ask questions.

One petroglyph site is reached by driving onto the reservation on State Highway 87-93 from Chandler; at the reservation boundary, keep to the left on State 87. Ten miles farther, turn left onto the old road marked by a sign to Oldberg Trading Post, and follow it for 2 miles. You'll find hundreds of rock carvings on basalt boulders on both sides of the dirt road after it enters a canyon beyond the trading post.

To reach Sacaton, turn right onto State Highway 187 where it branches off State 87. In March a 25-acre fairground at Sacaton is the site of the annual Pima tribal fair, *Mul-Chu-Tha*—Pima for "gathering of the people." The all-Indian event includes Indian games, dances, a rodeo, a museum, and Indian villages.

In the northwestern part of the Gila River reservation is the St. Johns Mission and Indian School. Perpetuation of the students' tribal ceremonial dances is encouraged at the school, located at Komatke about 17 miles southwest of Phoenix (51st Avenue and Williams Field Road). A two-day festival is held early in March.

PAPAGO INDIAN RESERVATION

Scattered across lonely stretches of cactus country and bunchgrass prairies in the Papago Indian Reservation are clusters of flat-roofed brown adobe houses—the villages of the Desert People. Some 5,000 Papagos live here; another 9,000 live off the reservation.

Most of the Papago villages are similar in appearance. You will see some mesquite and ocotillo corrals (called "living fences" because occasionally the posts take root again), perhaps some modern buildings, and a church—sometimes a small, flat-roofed stone chapel, sometimes a more elaborate structure. The village may be spread out over a mile or so rather than being a compact community. Only nine of the 74 inhabited Papago settlements have populations of more than 100—Ali Chukson, Topawa, Quijotoa, Gu Achi, Gu Vo, Pisinimo, Gu Oidah, Sells, and Chuichu. Sells, the largest, is the center of Papago activities and the meeting place for the 22-member elected tribal council.

Besides the main reservation—the second largest in the country—the Papagos have small reservations to the east and northwest. The San Xavier Indian Reservation (see page 77) is just southwest of Tucson, and the tiny Gila Bend Indian Reservation is directly north of the town of Gila Bend. One point of interest near the Gila Bend Reservation is Painted Rocks Historic Park, one of the state's best preserved collections of prehistoric Indian petroglyphs; about 15 miles west of Gila Bend, turn north from Interstate Highway 8 at the sign for Painted Rocks Dam and follow the paved road for 10 miles to where a sign directs you left onto a ¼-mile dirt road.

State Highway 86 cuts across the main reservation from east to west, connecting Tucson and Ajo. Another paved highway branches off State 86 at Quijotoa and goes north to Casa Grande, so you can reach the reservation by all-paved routes from either Phoenix or Tucson. If you're at home on desert roads, you will find the many offshoots from these highways inviting. Inquire locally about current road conditions. It's a good idea to carry water.

There are few restrictions on the use of roads and trails on the reservation, other than those of

CHURCH is most substantial building in many Papago villages. Ocotillo fence fronts this one at Chuichu.

courtesy to the people who live here. As you travel about, you may come upon seemingly deserted ramadas, dwellings, even whole villages; they are only temporarily unoccupied—don't enter closed buildings or disturb property.

Contemporary Papago life

Screen doors and glass windows on the houses, cars and pickup trucks in the yards, and watering troughs of concrete are visible evidence of the modern ways which the Papagos have adopted, as are the everyday clothing styles. Still, some old customs survive, and the older generation especially clings to a more traditional way of life. The Papago language is spoken in a majority of homes, though English is universally spoken by the younger generation and is the only language of tribal publications. You may still see some horse-drawn wooden wagons used for hauling wood, along with the more popular pickup trucks. Such age-old practices as the gathering and processing of mesquite beans, wild grains, and the fruit of the organ-pipe cactus and saguaro still are part of reservation life.

The Spanish and Mexican influence always has been strong. Spanish music is played at the dances held nearly every Saturday night somewhere on the reservation. Spanish missionaries were the first Europeans to live among the Papagos, and early each October thousands of Indians make a pilgrimage across the Mexican border to Magdalena, where Father Kino died.

Cattle-raising and some farming are the mainstays of the reservation economy, though many Papagos work off the reservation. One recently-developed program is a livestock camp where Papago youths are taught fundamentals of ranching.

Accommodations and camping

There are no overnight tourist accommodations on the Papago reservation, but you can make one-day trips onto the reservation from Tucson, Casa Grande, Ajo, or the campground at Organ Pipe Cactus National Monument. Supplies can be purchased at trading posts in Sells, Topawa, Quijotoa (Covered Wells), San Simon, and Gu Achi (Santa Rosa); there are two restaurants in Sells.

While there are no developed campsites on the reservation, you may camp at any unoccupied spot if you obtain a permit from the Tribal Office in Sells (50 cents per night).

Hunting

Rabbit, quail, and dove hunting is permitted on the reservation. Federal and state game laws and seasons apply, and you need a reservation hunting permit in addition to an Arizona license. Reservation permits must be obtained at the Tribal Office in Sells.

The community of Sells

In the middle of the reservation, ringed by dark gray mountains, is the seat of Papago tribal government. Sells, located just off State 86, is a community of both modern buildings and the traditional sod-roofed adobe brick houses. If you need information, go to the Tribal Office or to the government's Papago Agency across the street. In front of the Tribal Office building is a garden containing many varieties of cactus plants.

The Papago Tribal Arts and Crafts store on Main Street, opposite the Post Office, is part of the tribe's "self-help" program. The store is open from 8:30 A.M. to 4:30 P.M. weekdays.

In late October or November the annual three-day Papago All-Indian Rodeo and Fair attracts thousands of spectators to Sells. Besides the rodeo events there are exhibits of basketry and pottery, a parade, Papago singing and dancing, and a "Miss Papago" pageant. Admission for a full day's events is $2.50 for general admission, $4 for reserved seats, and 50 cents for children 6 to 12 years. For more information contact the Papago Rodeo and Fair Commission, Box 277, Sells, Arizona 85634.

The Roman Catholic church at Sells is the center of activity for the Feast of St. Francis in early October. After a service at the church (the sermon is in the musical Papago language), the feast is served up at the barbecue area on the church grounds. Dancing and games precede an evening of fireworks, and later Yaqui Indians from a small village near Tucson begin a religiously symbolic dance that may last until daylight.

Topawa Mission

Eight miles south of Sells you can see a Franciscan mission in operation. Brown-robed friars will show you through the Topawa Mission church and school, where Indian children from the surrounding desert are taught in their own language

ROUGHLY BUILT livestock pens of twisted mesquite dot reservation.

ENCAMPMENT for annual Feast of St. Francis at Sells still includes covered wagons, though cars and pickup trucks are now more common.

and in English. You reach Topawa via a paved road from Sells, and you pass through a magnificent saguaro cactus forest on the way.

East of Topawa is the great pointed monolith of Baboquivari Peak, 7,864 feet high. Its name means "with its beak in the air" in the Papago tongue. To reach Baboquivari Canyon you take a graded road east from Topawa for nine miles to an ungraded side road. (Don't drink the water in the canyon—it is likely to be contaminated.) From the canyon a trail climbs to the foot of the final 2,000-foot pinnacle.

Kitt Peak National Observatory

The gleaming white domes and instrument housings of Kitt Peak National Observatory are visible from Sells. The world's largest solar telescope is atop 6,875-foot-high Kitt Peak, 20 miles east of Sells and about 55 road miles west of Tucson.

One of three National Science Foundation astronomical research centers, the observatory contains 16, 36, 50, and 84-inch stellar telescopes in addition to the big solarscope. A 150-inch telescope will be installed by late 1971.

You drive up to the observatory on an 11½-mile paved road (State Highway 386) off State 86. At the visitor information center, interpretive displays explain the equipment and various astronomical phenomena. A gift shop here carries Papago crafts.

Kitt Peak is open to visitors daily (except Christmas Day) from 10 A.M. to 4 P.M. Admission is free. You should not begin the drive to the top later than about 2:30 P.M., as the road is closed at 4 P.M.

San Xavier Mission

Nine miles southwest of Tucson on the San Xavier Indian Reservation stands the twin-towered, whitewashed Mission San Xavier del Bac. A graceful blend of Moorish, Byzantine, and late Mexican Renaissance styles, the structure has been called the finest example of mission architecture in the United States.

Father Kino founded the mission in 1692, and it has been serving the Papago Indians ever since. The present church, called "White Dove of the Desert" because of its gleaming white exterior, has been in use since 1797.

Visitors are welcome any time between 6 A.M. and sunset. Twenty-minute lecture-tours are given every hour on the half-hour, from 9:30 A.M. to 4:30 P.M., Monday through Saturday. There is no admission fee; contributions are accepted.

Papago basketry is sold at a gift shop at the mission.

AT TOPAWA, nuns file from chapel to begin day of classes at school for Papago children. Plane brought Sunset reporters to the mission.

TUCSON

Just beyond the lands of the Papago Indians is the city of Tucson, where you can visit museum exhibits of Indian material, see a fort from the days of Apache wars, and shop for Indian crafts. You will find craft shops both downtown and in outlying districts; the choice of Papago basketry is good, but you also will see a variety of work from other tribes.

Fort Lowell

During the Apache campaigns of the 1870's and 1880's, Fort Lowell served as a base for detachments of cavalry and infantry and was the social center of the Tucson area. After the defeat of Geronimo in 1886, the fort declined in importance and finally was abandoned in 1891.

The former commanding officer's quarters have been restored and now contain a small museum, open from 10 A.M. to 4 P.M. Tuesday through Saturday, 2 to 4 P.M. Sunday; admission is free. The fort is located at the intersection of Fort Lowell and Craycroft roads, about 6 miles northeast of downtown Tucson.

Arizona State Museum

Exhibits at Arizona State Museum in Tucson range from the bones of a mammoth and the spear points that killed him some nine thousand years ago to modern Navajo, Apache, Papago, and Hopi arts and crafts. In between, chronologically, are artifacts from the Hohokam desert irrigation culture and the Anasazi pueblo villages of the plateau country farther north.

The museum is open from 10 A.M. to 5 P.M. Monday through Saturday, 2 to 5 P.M. Sunday. There is no admission charge. The museum is located just inside the University of Arizona campus at the corner of Park Avenue and University Boulevard.

Occasionally you can see Indian craftsmen demonstrating their specialties at the museum.

Arizona State Museum and the University of Arizona sponsor an archeological field school for college students at an Indian ruin site on the Fort Apache Indian Reservation.

BIBLIOGRAPHY

GENERAL

Atkinson, Mary J. *Indians of the Southwest.* San Antonio, Texas, Naylor Company, 1963. $5.00.

Bahti, Tom. *Southwestern Indian Tribes.* Flagstaff, Arizona, Northland Press, 1968. $5.00. Paperback, $2.00.

Ditzler, Robert E. *The Indian People of Arizona.* New York, Vantage Press, Inc., 1967. $3.75.

Dutton, Bertha P. *Indians of the Southwest.* Santa Fe, New Mexico, Southwestern Association on Indian Affairs, Inc., 1965. Paperback, $1.50.

Grant, Campbell. *Rock Art of the American Indian.* New York, Thomas Y. Crowell Company, 1967. $12.95.

Kidder, Alfred V. *An Introduction to the Study of Southwestern Archaeology.* New Haven, Connecticut, Yale University Press, 1962. $10.00. Paperback, $2.95.

Lange, Charles H., and Carroll L. Riley, editors. *The Southwestern Journals of Adolph F. Bandelier: 1880-82.* Albuquerque, University of New Mexico Press, 1966. $12.00.

McNitt, Frank. *The Indian Traders.* Norman, University of Oklahoma Press, 1962. $5.95.

Meriwether, David. *My Life in the Mountains and on the Plains.* Robert A. Griffen, editor. Norman, University of Oklahoma Press, 1965. $5.95.

Waters, Frank. *Masked Gods.* Chicago, Swallow Press, Inc., 1950. $8.50.

Wormington, H. M. *Prehistoric Indians of the Southwest.* Denver, Colorado, Denver Museum of Natural History, 1947. $3.00. Paperback, $2.00.

THE NAVAJOS

Gillmor, Frances, and Louise W. Wetherill. *Traders to the Navajos: The Story of the Wetherills of Kayenta.* Albuquerque, University of New Mexico Press, 1953. Paperback, $2.45.

Gilpin, Laura. *The Enduring Navaho.* Austin, University of Texas Press, 1968. $17.50. Photographic essay of Navajo people.

Jett, Stephen C., and Philip Hyde. *Navajo Wildlands.* San Francisco, Sierra Club Books, 1967. $25.00. Paperback, $3.95. Photographic essay of Navajo land.

Kluckhohn, Clyde, and Dorothea Leighton. *The Navaho.* Revised by Richard Kluckhohn and Lucy Wales. Garden City, New York, Anchor Doubleday, 1962. Paperback, $1.95.

LaFarge, Oliver. *Laughing Boy.* Boston, Houghton Mifflin Co., 1963. $5.95. Paperback, $1.95. A novel.

THE PUEBLOS

Bandelier, Adolf F. *The Delight Makers.* Indianapolis, Indiana, Dodd, Mead and Company, 1962. $5.00. A novel.

Benedict, Ruth. *Patterns of Culture.* Boston, Houghton Mifflin Co., 1961. $5.95. Paperback, $1.95.

Thompson, Laura, and Alice Joseph. *The Hopi Way.* New York, Russell & Russell Publishers, 1944. $8.50.

Tyler, Hamilton. *Pueblo Gods and Myths.* Norman, University of Oklahoma Press, 1964. $5.95.

Waters, Frank. *Book of the Hopi.* New York, The Viking Press, 1963. $10.00. Ballantine Books, Paperback, $1.25.
—*The Man Who Killed the Deer.* Chicago, Swallow Press, Inc., 1942. $5.00. Paperback, $2.50. A novel.

THE APACHES

Faulk, Odie B. *The Geronimo Campaign.* New York, Oxford University Press, 1969. $6.00.

Opler, Morris E. *An Apache Life Way.* New York, Cooper Square Publishers, Inc., 1941. $10.00.

Sonnichsen, C. L. *The Mescalero Apaches.* Norman, University of Oklahoma Press, 1958. $5.75.

THE PIMAS & THE PAPAGOS

Underhill, Ruth M. *The Papago Indians of Arizona and their Relatives the Pima.* Lawrence, Kansas, Bureau of Indian Affairs, Division of Education and Interior, Haskell Press, 1941. Paperback, 55 cents.
—*Singing for Power: The Song Magic of the Papago Indians of Southern Arizona.* Berkeley, University of California Press, 1969. $5.75.

Webb, George E. *A Pima Remembers.* Tucson, University of Arizona Press, 1959. $3.00.

THE HAVASUPAIS

Wampler, Joseph C. *Havasu Canyon: Gem of the Grand Canyon.* Box 45, Berkeley, Calif., 1959. Paperback, $2.50.

THE UTES

Rockwell, Wilson. *The Utes: A Forgotten People.* Chicago, Sage Books, 1956. Out of print.

ARTS & CRAFTS

Adair, John. *The Navajo and Pueblo Silversmiths.* Norman, University of Oklahoma Press, 1944. $5.95.

Cain, H. Thomas. *Pima Indian Basketry.* Phoenix, The Heard Museum of Anthropology and Primitive Arts, 1962. Paperback, $1.25.

Colton, Harold S. *Hopi Kachina Dolls.* Albuquerque, University of New Mexico Press, 1959. $7.50.

Dunn, Dorothy. *American Indian Painting of the Southwest and Plains Areas.* Albuquerque, University of New Mexico Press, 1968. $25.00.

Fewkes, Jesse W. *Hopi Katchinas Drawn by Native Artists.* Glorieta, New Mexico, Rio Grande Press, Inc., 1967. $15.00.

Field, Clark. *Indian Pottery of the Southwest Post Spanish Period.* Tulsa, Oklahoma, Philbrook Art Center, 1963. Paperback, $1.00.

Fontana, Bernard L., et al. *Papago Indian Pottery.* Seattle, University of Washington Press, 1962. $6.50.

Harlow, Francis. *Historic Pueblo Indian Pottery.* Santa Fe, Museum of New Mexico, 1969. Paperback, $1.00.

Harlow, Francis, and John Young. *Contemporary Pueblo Indian Pottery.* Santa Fe, Museum of New Mexico, 1965. Paperback, $1.00.

Kent, Kate P. *The Story of Navaho Weaving.* Phoenix, The Heard Museum of Anthropology and Primitive Arts, 1961. Paperback, $1.50.

Marriott, Alice. *Maria: The Potter of San Ildefonso.* Norman, University of Oklahoma Press, 1948. $4.95.

Tanner, Clara L. *Southwest Indian Craft Arts.* Tucson, University of Arizona Press, 1968. $15.00.

Reichard, Gladys. *Navajo Shepherd and Weaver: The Art and Technique of Navajo Weaving.* Glorieta, New Mexico, Rio Grande Press, Inc., 1968. $8.00.

Villaseñor, David V. *Tapestries in Sand: The Spirit of Indian Sandpainting.* Healdsburg, California, Naturegraph Company, 1966. $4.50. Paperback, $2.95.

Wright, Barton, and Evelyn Roat. *This Is a Hopi Kachina.* Flagstaff, Museum of Northern Arizona, 1962. Paperback, $1.00.

Index